CW01283095

# How to Make People Like You

*Psychological Tricks, Habits, and Jokes to Immediately Increase Your Charisma and Ability to Influence People*

© Copyright 2023 - All rights reserved.

The content contained within this book may not be reproduced, duplicated, or transmitted without direct written permission from the author or the publisher.

Under no circumstances will any blame or legal responsibility be held against the publisher, or author, for any damages, reparation, or monetary loss due to the information contained within this book, either directly or indirectly.

**Legal Notice:**

This book is copyright protected. It is only for personal use. You cannot amend, distribute, sell, use, quote or paraphrase any part of the content within this book without the consent of the author or publisher.

**Disclaimer Notice:**

Please note the information contained within this document is for educational and entertainment purposes only. All effort has been executed to present accurate, up-to-date, reliable, and complete information. No warranties of any kind are declared or implied. Readers acknowledge that the author is not engaging in the rendering of legal, financial, medical, or professional advice. The content within this book has been derived from various sources. Please consult a licensed professional before attempting any techniques outlined in this book.

By reading this document, the reader agrees that under no circumstances is the author responsible for any losses, direct or indirect, that are incurred as a result of the use of the information contained within this document, including, but not limited to, errors, omissions, or inaccuracies.

# Free Bonus from Andy Gardner

Hi!

My name is Andy Gardner, and first off, I want to THANK YOU for reading my book.

Now you have a chance to join my exclusive email list related to human psychology and self-development so you can get the ebook below for free as well as the potential to get more ebooks for free! Simply click the link below to join.

P.S. Remember that it's 100% free to join the list.

Access your free bonuses here:
**https://livetolearn.lpages.co/how-to-make-people-like-you-paperback/**

# Table of Contents

- INTRODUCTION ........................................................................... 1
- CHAPTER 1: SOCIAL CONNECTIONS: WHY ARE THEY SO IMPORTANT? ........................................................................ 3
- CHAPTER 2: HOW TO MAKE A GREAT FIRST IMPRESSION ............... 13
- CHAPTER 3: UNDERSTANDING AND UTILIZING BODY LANGUAGE ................................................................................ 22
- CHAPTER 4: HOW TO GAIN CONFIDENCE AND GET RESPECT ....... 31
- CHAPTER 5: INCREASE YOUR CHARISMA AND START TURNING HEADS! .................................................................... 44
- CHAPTER 6: 14 PSYCHOLOGICAL TRICKS TO INFLUENCE PEOPLE ..................................................................................... 53
- CHAPTER 7: THE ART OF LISTENING WITHOUT JUDGEMENT ........ 62
- CHAPTER 8: ASKING THE RIGHT QUESTIONS AT THE RIGHT TIME .......................................................................................... 74
- CHAPTER 9: TWELVE WAYS TO BE MORE INTERESTING ............... 83
- CHAPTER 10: DOS AND DON'TS WHEN IT COMES TO BEING LIKED ........................................................................................ 93
- CONCLUSION ............................................................................ 104
- HERE'S ANOTHER BOOK BY ANDY GARDNER THAT YOU MIGHT LIKE ............................................................................. 106
- FREE BONUS FROM ANDY GARDNER ..................................... 107
- REFERENCES ............................................................................ 108

# Introduction

Do you feel all alone? Do you want to learn how to make others like you?

Do you, as an introvert, find it challenging to make new friends or get the impression that no one likes you?

Do you want to be liked, valued, and recognized by others?

How much do you want to improve your self-assurance, charisma, and overall likeability?

Is the idea of a better, more convenient, and more fulfilling life appealing to you?

If any of these questions describe you, you are not alone. In this fast-paced and digitally connected world, we are more physically isolated than ever. Reasons are varied - people are busy, or you might have bought into the carefully curated social media posts that almost everyone indulges in, which we know are not a true reflection of ordinary lives.

Even so, it is a real problem, and this book will teach you how to deal with it so that you no longer have to suffer from FOMO.

The ability to meet new people quickly and easily could have far-reaching consequences in your personal and professional lives. Whether your goal is to advance your career or simply meet interesting people in a new location, this skill is worth developing.

Everyone has met someone who they immediately like. Despite their lack of effort, they have become like a best-selling novel that has been well received by readers everywhere. You can tell right away that you can trust this person.

Maybe it's the CEO of the company you worked for whose magnetic personality is the key to its continued success. Or perhaps you know someone who can walk into a party and leave with a couple of friends without even trying. The real mystery is how they became so popular. Do you believe you can learn to make others like you?

Not everyone is born with the skill of making new friends. Despite this, we can all improve our likeability. With some guidance, you can start developing routines that will enhance your social interactions with others.

The fundamentals of making others like you are self-evident: be pleasant, courteous, and a good human being. There are less obvious and covert things you can do that will significantly impact how others see you.

The solution is at your fingertips. With this book, you will embark on a one-of-a-kind self-improvement journey to learn how to become a more lovable and appealing person. You won't find a more approachable book than this one, and its practical advice sets it apart from the competition.

Even though the process requires experience and confidence, those with tried-and-true strategies and detailed walkthroughs will find the journey easy.

# Chapter 1: Social Connections: Why Are They So Important?

Sorry introverts, but having social connections is good for your mental health and well-being. According to Mental Health UK, recent studies have found that social connections can significantly impact a person's mental health. Living in a community and being close to your family and friends can make you happier and improve your physical health. Healthy relationships can make you live longer because they protect you from mental issues and risks that can decrease your lifespan. Some people make the mistake of thinking that social connections are all about quantity rather than quality — the type of relationships you have in your life matter more than the number. Surrounding yourself with toxic people can have the opposite effect on your mental well-being. Negative social connections increase anxiety and the risk of depression.

Making social connections is important because it allows you grow.
*https://www.pexels.com/photo/group-of-friends-singing-while-sitting-on-beach-sand-7149165/*

Most people pay attention to what they eat, their lifestyle, and their sleeping habits and forget that relationships are also essential to one's well-being. Therefore, when establishing connections, focus on people who make you feel good after spending time with them, not the ones who leave you drained and stressed. Building solid and uncomplicated connections will play a huge role in regulating your mental health. Positive relationships make you a better person, boosting your self-confidence, improving your quality of life, and making you more trusting and empathetic. People going through any sort of recovery also need to be surrounded by their loved ones, as it can speed up their healing process. Strong relationships can also boost the immune system and lower the risk of dementia.

Human beings aren't meant to live alone. Since ancient times, people have understood that living in groups is vital for survival, and this is how and why tribes evolved. Thousands of years later, science has confirmed what ancient people knew all along - social connections are necessary. During the COVID-19 pandemic, when people were isolated and forced to stay at home, many suffered from mental health issues. Even introverts struggle with isolation and miss having a real human connection.

Imagine having a bad day at work. You are overworking, your boss never seems to appreciate you, and you feel stressed. You send a text message to your workgroup saying, "I had the worst day at work today. I can't take it anymore." Seconds later, you get a message from three of your work friends saying they feel your pain and suggesting you all go out after work to vent together. You go to a nice restaurant, have a delicious meal, and spend the whole night talking, laughing, and having fun. You go home feeling a load has been lifted off your shoulders. Your job is still horrible, but you aren't as stressed or angry as you used to be, thanks to having a healthy support group at work.

Social connections will make your life better. This chapter will explain their value and how they can benefit your life.

## What Are Social Connections?

Social connections are the relationships you cultivate with the people in your life, whether your family members, friends, co-workers, neighbors, etc. You don't have to be close friends with all your social connections. Some relationships can be casual. The size of your social circle is also immaterial. Most people assume that you should have a vast number of social connections, with hundreds of friends on Facebook and thousands of followers on Instagram and LinkedIn. You can have hundreds of friends on your contact list, and none of them will come through if you need help. Having a couple of close friends who support, love, and respect you is enough. It doesn't matter how many people you have around you. What matters is how they make you *feel*.

Social connection in a community is living in a place where you don't feel like a stranger. You belong there. You know your neighbors and the people in your community. You have a healthy support group and are surrounded by individuals with whom you can build strong and healthy relationships.

Human beings are social by nature. From the moment you are born, you connect instantly with your parents and siblings, and as you grow older, you keep forming new connections. The first bond you form with your parents impacts the rest of your relationships. Having loving and caring parents will influence your choice of the people you spend time with as you will gravitate more toward healthy relationships. According to the research conducted by Matthew Lieberman (author, social psychologist at UCLA, and founding editor of the journal, *Social Cognitive and Affective Neuroscience)*, human beings crave interaction; we are wired to form connections with others.

# Elements of Social Connection

Understanding social connection requires you to have a full grasp of its elements.

### Belonging

Everyone wants to feel like they belong. The concept of social connection has always been associated with the feeling of belonging, being a part of a group, and being around people similar to you. Developing social connections stems from a deep psychological need to connect with one another, contributing to your quality of life.

Connecting with others and feeling that they care about you, respect you, and value you can make you feel that you belong. Everyone wants to feel that they belong somewhere. Again, this relates to our evolution and how our ancestors created tribes to feel they were a part of a community. You make friends, attend church, spend time with family members, and try to make your co-workers like you so you can feel a part of a community. A sense of belonging can protect you from loneliness and isolation and make you more resilient.

There is a difference between feeling alone and lonely. Neither is associated with the number of people in your life. You can have hundreds of connections or be around a dozen people and feel lonely if you don't find any of these relationships fulfilling. However, being alone is when you aren't around people, but you don't feel lonely because the relationships in your life are fulfilling, even if you only have two friends.

### Support

Support is an essential element in social connections. People establish relationships to feel supported by their loved ones. Social support involves a person or group helping you solve a problem or achieve a goal. There are various types of social support. The first is emotional support which is seen s in intimate connections, but you can experience it in other kinds of connections. It involves providing love, understanding, and sympathy.

Informational support is supporting someone by providing helpful information, like telling a friend about a job vacancy or providing valuable advice for a relationship issue or medical advice.

Instrumental support is the last type of support that is more practical, like lending a friend money.

### Socializing

Socializing is engaging in activities with other people, like watching a movie, going out for dinner, or attending a concert. These activities allow you to spend time with your loved ones or with co-workers so you can bond. Many activities are more fun when you do them with other people.

## Types of Social Connections

You don't just randomly choose people to be in your social circle. Social connections are based on certain criteria; thus, various types exist. Understanding these types is necessary as you expand your social circle and form new connections.

### Intimate Connections

Intimate connections aren't the same as sexual ones. According to psychologist Megan Fleming, intimate connections involve deep, intense closeness with someone. You don't form this right away - it develops over time. When you achieve it, that person becomes your *comfort zone*. And this type of connection doesn't occur only between romantic partners; you can develop it with your family members, friends, co-workers, etc. Intimacy can happen when you connect emotionally, intellectually, spiritually, and - in the case of romantic partners - physically.

### Relational Connections

Relational connections occur when you relate to others and form healthy relationships with people you enjoy being around. Whether it's friends, co-workers, or family members, these people have a common interest or activity, making engaging with them easy. For instance, by forming relational connections with your co-workers, you'll all work well together as a team and come up with creative solutions for your problems.

### Collective Connection

A collective connection usually involves a group of people who share a direct or indirect bond. It can refer to people sharing similar backgrounds or cultures. For instance, Americans working abroad usually connect with other Americans since they share a common bond which is their home country.

## The Importance of Good Social Connections

Social connections are necessary for our survival. Humans are born with the need to connect; it's in our DNA. When babies are born, they cry for their mothers. Even though they don't understand how the world works, they are driven by the urge to connect with their caregiver. The same applied to ancient societies that didn't have the scientific research we have now, but they understood the need to live in groups. Their tribal instincts kicked in as they found that tribal living gave them support, protection, and an identity. Historic movies and tv-shows have shown us how families lived together in the same house and cared for one another. It didn't matter if the house was big or small; nothing could keep close family members apart.

Being sociable gives you confidence.
https://www.pexels.com/photo/group-of-friends-sitting-near-lifeguard-post-7148441/

Things have changed in the modern world; not only do people move out when they reach a certain age, but some family members can spend years without seeing each other. Most people have busy schedules that don't have time to connect with their loved ones. Even in the age of social networks that are supposed to make us feel more connected, we have never felt further apart. Your friends and family create WhatsApp chat groups to help everyone "connect" with one another. However, how can you connect with someone behind a screen? Scientists have found many people feel lonely and isolated now more than ever.

Isolation and loneliness don't drive people to go out there and find meaningful connections. On the contrary, they make you feel stuck as you get accustomed to these feelings and struggle with forming bonds with others. Negative emotions attract more negative emotions, which impact your mental and physical fitness and disrupt other areas of your life, like your work performance.

Do you remember how you felt when other kids didn't want to play with you when you were a child? Scientists have found that negative social interactions and rejections have the same impact on the brain as physical pain. You don't only need social connections, but you need positive and healthy relationships.

Healthy connections can change the way you view the world around you. Imagine two people in a hospital; one has their family and friends by their side supporting them, while the other has a room full of flowers but not one person around. How do you think each one is feeling about themselves and the world? Being alone during a critical time like this can impact a person's healing, as they will probably take longer to recover than those surrounded by their loved ones. According to author Shawn Achor (Harvard), if you are climbing a hill alone, you will consider it 30% steeper than climbing it with a friend. In other words, people feel they can get through challenges and hard times when they have a friend or a support group by their side.

A lack of social connections in your life can seriously affect your physical health. It can raise the sugar levels in your blood to dangerous levels, cause inflammation, raise your blood pressure, impact your immune system, and increase the risk of cancer and cardiovascular diseases. In some severe cases, it can lead to suicidal thoughts.

## Other Benefits of Good Social Connections
### Increase Your Lifespan
According to a 2016 University of North Carolina study, loneliness and isolation can shorten your lifespan and lead to early death. A lack of social connection is more dangerous to your health than smoking and obesity. Even if you don't see your social circle often or you don't talk every day, knowing they are there and supporting you is enough to make you feel better and healthier, which can increase your

lifespan. Longevity, in this sense, isn't associated with a certain age or gender. Anyone can benefit from good social connections in their lives.

### Make Your Life Better

Lack of social connection can harm your emotional health as well. According to a 2018 study conducted by the American Chemical Society, isolation can increase the risk of obesity, stroke, and smoking. Positive social connections will improve your quality of life and make you happier.

### Increase Your Resilience

Being surrounded by supportive people, especially after a traumatic experience, can increase your resilience and help you get back on your feet faster. When you are going through a rough time, you will be stressed and consumed with negative thoughts and emotions. Switching your perspective or seeing the glass half full can be impossible when you are only focused on negativity. A good friend can cheer you up, lift your spirits, and change your outlook. Challenges don't seem so big when you know you aren't facing them alone. Your social circle gives meaning to your life, which also increases your resilience.

### Increase Your Self-Confidence

Everyone has negative thoughts and an internal critic that can sometimes destroy self-confidence. Good friends and supportive family members can make you feel better about yourself, silence your inner critic, and boost your self-confidence. Feeling loved and appreciated is necessary for your well-being and can increase your self-worth. You feel valuable when someone cares about you and makes you feel loved and needed. It also reinforces the feeling of belonging, which can make you thrive and improve other parts of your life. Your support group makes you feel secure and supported. Knowing that someone will always have your back and be there for you whenever you need them can give you the confidence and strength to withstand any challenges.

### Social Connections and Mental Health

The COVID-19 pandemic proved that our mental health suffers without human connection. Loneliness can increase the risk of multiple issues like depression and anxiety. Social connections make you feel that you belong. For instance, if you get a lucrative job offer abroad, you will not jump at the opportunity immediately because the thought of leaving your loved ones behind is so difficult. Your home isn't a *place*; it's where your friends and family are. When moving to a new place, a person first connects with the people in their community to feel less alone and isolated. Human connection makes things easier. Whether going through a breakup or losing someone close, knowing you have someone to rely on and connect with can take a load off of you.

**Feelings of Fulfillment**

Imagine getting a phone call from your high school best friend, whom you haven't seen or heard from in years. You get together and find yourself hugging them and crying tears of joy for finally reuniting with an old friend. In another scenario, your friends come over with food and drinks, and each of you spends your time venting about work or relationships. In the last scenario, you and your friends from work go out for dinner, where you have fun, make jokes, and laugh. In the three scenarios, you expressed different emotions, which makes the brain release the happy chemical dopamine, so each event leaves you feeling lighter and fulfilled. Whether it is tears or laughter, releasing emotions can improve your mood. Cultivating healthy connections at work can also make you feel more fulfilled in your job, which will enhance your performance and productivity.

**Decrease Suicidal Thoughts**

It isn't an exaggeration to say that human connections can save your life. As mentioned, they are vital for your survival. Loneliness can lead to depression which is known to increase suicidal thoughts. Healthy relationships can make you supported, heard, and less alone, which can prevent suicidal thoughts. It will also provide you with someone to talk to and guide you in your darkest times.

Life is demanding enough without having people by your side to support you. Remember, love and support go both ways. Cultivating social connections requires you to also support and accept the people in your life. Relationships are about giving and taking – and if you take without giving, your relationships will suffer. Give the people in your life a safe space to vent about their problems and help them find solutions when needed – or just provide a sympathetic ear.

We all want to love and be loved in return which is one of the reasons we seek human connection. Human beings were put on this earth to socialize. Nothing can ever replace human connection. Even if you aren't social, you will still need someone to have your back and be by your side during hard times. Everyone needs help sometimes. Even the worst and most miserable situations can be easier with a friend by your side. Remember, misery loves company.

Increasing social connections or widening your circle requires meeting people and making new friends. If you want people to like you, focus on creating a solid first impression. It can take someone less than a minute to decide whether they like you. You only have a few seconds to make a powerful and great impression. This isn't as complicated as you think. Head to the next chapter to discover how you can make a lasting first impression that will guarantee everyone you meet will never forget you.

# Chapter 2: How to Make a Great First Impression

We've all heard the saying that first impressions are everything. And while it's true that first impressions are important, there's a lot of psychology and science behind *why* they're so important. For starters, our brains are wired to make snap judgments about people based on very little information. In fact, research has shown that we form first impressions in as little as one-tenth of a second. This ability to size someone up quickly is an evolutionary adaptation that helped our ancestors survive in the wild by quickly identifying whether someone was a friend or foe.

First impressions leave a mark on people.
*https://unsplash.com/photos/9cd8qOgcNIY*

These days, thankfully, we don't have to worry about being eaten by tigers or other predators. But how our brains work means that first impressions still significantly impact how we see people. Once we form an initial opinion about someone, we tend to filter all future information about them through that lens. So, if we have a positive first impression of someone, we're more likely to see them in a positive light going forward. Similarly, if we have a negative first impression, we're more likely to view them negatively continuously.

There are a few things you can do to make sure you make a great first impression. Firstly, dress appropriately for the situation - whether *business casual* for a job interview or your *best party outfit* for a night out. Secondly, pay attention to your body language and be aware of how you're coming across - confidence is the key. Finally, try to be yourself and let your personality shine through - people are attracted to authenticity.

Making a great first impression is essential to getting ahead in life. By understanding the psychology behind why first impressions matter, you can learn how to make sure you always put your best foot forward.

## What Is a First Impression?

A first impression is the initial judgment t a person forms about someone else. It happens when we meet someone for the first time and can be based on their appearance, body language, tone of voice, or how they are dressed. First impressions are often made very quickly - within seconds of meeting someone - and can be challenging to change. The old saying goes that you only have one chance to make a good first impression. Although we may not realize it, we often form first impressions without even thinking. That's because our brain constantly tries to process the barrage of information it encounters and make split-second judgments about what it means. In fact, studies have shown that people usually decide whether they like someone or not within seconds of meeting them. While first impressions are often based on superficial factors, there is some psychology behind them. For example, research has shown that people tend to judge others based on their level of attractiveness. Good-looking people are often perceived as more successful, happy, and intelligent. There is also some evidence that people mimic each other's body language when they first meet, which creates a rapport between them. First impressions are not always accurate, but they can be difficult to change once they are formed. That's why you need to be aware of the impression you make on others and to try to put your best foot forward when meeting new people.

## Why Is the First Impression so Important?

It's been said that you never get a second chance to make a first impression. This is especially true when it comes to job interviews. In today's competitive job market, the interview process has become increasingly significant, and making a good first impression is often the difference between getting the job and being passed over.

There are several reasons the first impression is so important. For one, it sets the tone for the rest of the interview. If you make an excellent first impression, the interviewer will be more likely to see you in a positive light and ask you questions designed to elicit more positive responses. On the other hand, if you make a terrible first impression, the interviewer may spend the rest of the interview trying to recover from it. In addition, first impressions are often based on nonverbal cues such as body language and tone of voice. These cues can be just as vital as what you actually say, and they can give the interviewer an idea of your personality and whether or not you would be a good fit for the company.

Finally, remember first impressions are often made before you even open your mouth. The way you dress, your posture, and your general demeanor can all contribute to the first impression you make. For this reason, take some time to prepare for your interview well ahead of the date to make the best possible impression on your potential employer.

## What Is a Bad First Impression?

A bad first impression can have far-reaching effects that linger even after one is no longer in the other person's presence. Leaving a poor impact on someone might result from a variety of different things, such as weak communication skills, a lack of confidence or enthusiasm, or even simply the subconscious association that another may have with certain physical characteristics. When making an impression on others, be mindful and aware of your body language, attitude, and words – so it is successful. A negative mindset can quickly become apparent, creating an unfavorable atmosphere and leading to instant rejection by the other party. In fact, studies show that we make snap decisions about others within the first seconds of meeting them. And once we've formed an opinion, it's hard to change it. All of this means that making a good first impression is essential if you want to be successful in life. But how exactly can you avoid making a bad impression?

People judge others based on appearance, body language, and behavior. You'll likely leave a negative impression if you look unkempt, slouchy, or hostile. Similarly, if you seem nervous or shy, people may not take the time to get to know you better. It's also critical to watch what you say and do since others will remember it if you offend them with your words or actions. Finally, remember that first impressions are often subjective – so even if you think you made a great first impression, there's always a chance that the other person didn't feel the same way.

## How Do I Make a Good First Impression?

### 1. Be on Time

Anyone who's ever been on a first date knows the importance of making a good first impression. And while there are lots of ways to do this, the top of the list and easiest to do is simply being on time. Why is this? Well, it turns out there's some psychology behind it.

When we meet someone new, our brain automatically tries to size them up and determine if they're trustworthy. Part of this process involves looking for cues that tell us whether or not the person is reliable. And one of the most prominent cues we look for is whether or not they're *punctual*. After all, if someone can't even show up on time for a first date, how reliable are they likely to be in other areas of their life? Being late sends the message that you don't respect other people's time, which makes you seem selfish and unreliable.

On the other hand, being on time (or even early) shows that you're willing to go out of your way to ensure things run smoothly and value other people's time as much as yours. So, if you want to make a good first impression, show up on time (or even a little early). It'll send the right message and help put your date at ease.

Being on time leaves a lasting good impression on others.
*https://unsplash.com/photos/otjiUhq5Zcw*

## 2. Establish Good Eye Contact

When meeting someone for the first time, part of adding to the person's opinion is how much eye contact you make. Eye contact conveys confidence and interest and helps establish a connection with the other person. When you meet someone new, take a moment to look them in the eye and give them a sincere smile. This sends the message that you are confident and interested in getting to know them better. You may also want to extend a hand for a handshake, which is another nonverbal way to show your enthusiasm. It also sends a nonverbal message that you are paying attention and engaged in the conversation. In addition, making eye contact can help to put the other person at ease and make them feel more comfortable talking to you. So, if you want to make an excellent first impression, keep your eyes on the prize. Making eye contact is one of the easiest and most effective ways to make a great first impression.

## 3. Have a Winning Smile (But Not a Fake One!)

Everyone is aware of the significance of first impressions. You want to put your best foot forward when you meet someone new. One of the easiest ways to do this is simply to smile. Smiling is a potent nonverbal cue that conveys a lot of information. For one thing, it conveys friendliness and approachability. Smiling is one of the universal forms of nonverbal communication, and it conveys a range of emotions, from happiness and amusement to love and interest. It's also an incredibly powerful tool for making first impressions. When you smile at someone, they're more likely to smile back, which in turn makes them feel good. And when people feel good around you, they're more likely to associate positive traits with you, such as being friendly, trustworthy, and competent.

It makes you seem like someone who is easy to talk to and who would be pleasant to spend time with. Smiling can also make you seem more competent and trustworthy. In other words, when you smile, you're making yourself more likable - and seeming like someone worth their time.

So why does smiling have such a powerful effect? Part of it has to do with biology. When we see someone smiling, it triggers the release of dopamine in our brains, which makes us feel happy. When we smile, our facial muscles are responsible for producing positive emotions are activated. In other words, when we smile, we actually end up feeling happier and more positive overall. So next time you're meeting someone new, remember to turn that frown upside down and give them your best smile! So, if you want to make a great first impression, don't forget to smile. It might seem like a small thing, but it can go a long way in helping others see you in a positive light.

### 4. Use Positive Body Language

When you meet someone for the first time, what do you notice about them? Chances are, you pay attention to their body language first. Studies have shown that we judge others based on their body language within the first few seconds of meeting them. This means that making a good first impression is essential to form positive relationships with others. So, what can you do to ensure you put your best foot forward? One of the key things is to use positive body language. This includes maintaining eye contact, smiling, and having an open posture. Negative body language, however, includes things like crossing your arms, looking down, and avoiding eye contact.

Positive body language signals to the other person that you're interested in them and what they have to say. It also makes you appear more confident and approachable. On the other hand, negative body language can make you seem disinterested, unconfident, and even hostile. It might seem like simple advice, but these small gestures can go a long way in making a good impression. When we smile, for example, it triggers a release of endorphins in the brain, making us feel happy and more attractive to others.

Similarly, maintaining eye contact signals that we are interested in the other person and makes them feel valued. Finally, an open posture indicates that we are approachable and trustworthy. In summary, by using positive body language, we create an instant rapport with others and set the stage for a lasting relationship.

### 5. Be Empathetic

Empathy is the ability to understand and share the feelings of another person. It's about being able to see things from their perspective and having a deep understanding of their emotions. When you're empathizing with someone, you're not just listening to what they're saying; you're also trying to feel what they're feeling. This can be a powerful way to connect with someone and build rapport.

One of the easiest ways to show empathy is simply reflecting on what the other person is saying. This lets them know that you're hearing and understanding them. You can also ask questions to learn more about their experiences and how they're feeling. For example, you might say, "That sounds really tough. How are you managing?" Active listening, or paying full attention to what someone is saying without interruption, is another way to show empathy. This involves making eye contact, maintaining an open body posture, and periodically nodding or affirming.

When you take the time to be empathetic with others, it sends the message that you care about them and are interested in hearing what they have to say. It's a great way to build relationships and create a positive impression.

### 6. Dress for the Occasion

Whether you're going on a first date, interviewing for a job, or attending a party, it's crucial to make a strong first impression. And one of the easiest ways is to dress for the occasion. For example, if you're meeting someone for coffee, you probably don't need to wear a three-piece suit. But dressing professionally is a good idea if you're going to a job interview. Wearing the right clothes sends a message that you're taking the situation seriously and respecting the person or people you're meeting. It can also boost your confidence, which is a big part of making a good impression. So next time you've got a meeting or event, take some time to think about what you'll wear. Dressing for the occasion is a small but effective way to ensure you put your best foot forward. Dressing for the occasion can go a long way toward making a great first impression.

### 7. Be Yourself

Being authentic means being honest about who you are and what you believe in. It means being genuine in your interactions and staying true to your values and principles. People can sense when you're being fake or trying to put on an act, and it comes across as insincere. On the other hand, when you're being authentic, people can see that you're genuine, and that's much more appealing. When you're being honest, people can see the real you, which can help build trust and rapport. Authenticity is also essential for building lasting relationships. After all, how can you truly connect with someone if you're not being honest about who you are? So next time you're in a situation where you want to make a good impression, forget about trying to put on an act. Just be yourself, and let the world see the amazing person that you are.

### 8. Do Your Research

One of the best ways to make a lasting first impression is to do your research for the occasion. This shows that you are taking the time to learn about the other person and are interested in making a good impression. For example, suppose you are meeting someone for a business meeting. In that case, you should research their company and the industry they work in. This will give you something to talk about and show you are prepared. When meeting someone for a social occasion, you should research their interests to find common ground. This will make the conversation flow more smoothly, and the other person will feel more comfortable. Taking the time to do your research shows that you care about making a good impression and are willing to put in the effort to do so.

### 9. Put Your Phone Away

In today's age, it's becoming increasingly common for people to rely on their phones for just about everything. From directions to checking the time, our phones have become an extension of ourselves. However, when meeting someone new, you must put your phone away and give the person your full attention. There are a few reasons for this. First, it shows that you're interested in what the other person has to say. Second, it can help prevent awkward moments if you accidentally drop your phone or receive a notification during the conversation. Finally, it sends the message that you're present in the moment and that you value the person's company. So next time you're meeting someone new, remember to put your phone away and make a great first impression.

### 10. Listen More Than You Speak

People love to talk about themselves. It's human nature. So, by letting the other person do most of the talking, you not only come across as a good listener but also learn more about them. What they like, what they don't like, their hobbies, etc. And all of this information can help determine whether or not there is a potential connection. Listening also shows that you respect the other person and their opinion. It shows that you value their thoughts and ideas and are interested in hearing what they have to say. This can go a long way in building rapport and trust.

### 11. Be Open but Confident

First impressions are important, but they can be challenging to control. You want to be open and friendly but don't want to come across as desperate or too eager. The key is to strike the right balance between being confident and being approachable. One way to do this is to make eye contact and smile when you meet someone new. This shows that you're interested in getting to know them, but it also conveys confidence. Another way to make a great first impression is to be upbeat. This doesn't mean you have to be over-the-top happy, but it does mean avoiding negativity. Finally, remember that first impressions are just that - first impressions. Don't obsess over them too much. Just relax and be yourself, and you will make a great impression.

Now that you know what makes a good first impression . . . *follow this advice*. The next time you meet someone new, make sure to smile, make eye contact, and give a firm handshake. And don't forget to keep your appearance neat and polished. Offer a handshake, introduce yourself, and make small talk. By following these simple tips, you can make sure that you always put your best foot forward.

# Chapter 3: Understanding and Utilizing Body Language

Most of us are unaware that our bodies can reveal a lot about our personalities. By observing someone's body language, you can often tell if they are confident or shy, extroverted or introverted, etc. Of course, you must consider the context in which someone is exhibiting a particular behavior. For example, someone who is typically very outgoing may act differently if they are in a large group of strangers. However, body language can be a reliable indicator of someone's personality.

Body language says a lot about your intentions and mood.
*https://unsplash.com/photos/mSzCl0H4beY*

Several common body language cues can clue you into what a person is feeling. For example, people comfortable with themselves and others have an open posture, with their arms and legs uncrossed. They also make eye contact and smile frequently. On the other hand, someone uneasy in social situations may have closed off body language, such as crossing their arms or legs or avoiding eye contact. Another giveaway is fidgeting - people who are anxious or uncomfortable tend to fidget more than those who are relaxed.

Of course, it is crucial to remember that everyone is unique and that any number of things can affect someone's body language. However, if you pay attention to the cues mentioned above, you'll get a pretty good idea of what kind of person someone is - even if they don't say a word!

## What Can Our Body Language Reveal?

### 1. Thoughts

When it comes to understanding someone's thoughts, words are only part of the equation. Our body language provides valuable clues about what we're really thinking and can be challenging to control. For example, if we're interested in someone, we might unintentionally lean in or make more eye contact than usual. Conversely, we might cross our arms or avoid eye contact altogether if we feel defensive. Paying attention to these subtle cues can give us a much better sense of what someone is thinking, even when they're trying to hide it. Before making judgments, it's vital to consider body language cues and other background indicators because they can be easily misread. However, when used correctly, they can be a powerful tool for reading people's thoughts.

Body language is a form of non-verbal communication wherein information is represented or communicated through physical activities instead of words. These activities include body posture, eye movement, facial expressions, touch, gestures, and space utilization. Animals and humans both exhibit body language, but we'll concentrate on how humans use body language to portray their emotions. It is thought that body language makes up the majority of our nonverbal communication; however, it is often misinterpreted or not given much attention. The wrong body language can create anxiety, confusion, and even hostility. It can also be used to interpret a person's inner dialogue through cues such as facial expressions, postures, and gestures. By paying attention to these hints, we can better understand how someone is feeling, what they are thinking, their inner dialogue and what they might be trying to communicate. Interpretations of body language can vary depending on culture and context; however, some universal cues tend to have the same meaning across cultures. For example, touching one's face or nose is often a sign of deception; while averting one's gaze is often a sign of shame or guilt. When analyzing body language, context is crucial because some indicators might signify several things, as some cues can have multiple meanings. For example, folding one's arms across the chest can indicate *defensiveness or confidence.* To accurately interpret someone's body language, you must consider the situation and all other nonverbal cues that are present. Paying attention to body language can help us better understand the inner dialogue between others and ourselves.

## 2. The Emotional State

Body language can be used to decipher a person's emotional state, as well as to communicate emotions. For example, crossed arms may indicate that a person is feeling defensive or uncomfortable, while an open posture may signal that they are relaxed and approachable. Facial expressions are cues to emotions, with smiles and laughter indicating happiness, while furrowed brows and clenched jaws can convey anger or frustration. By paying attention to these and other cues, we can better understand how someone is feeling, which can be helpful in personal and professional interactions.

## 3. The Intentions

Most people are not aware of the significance of body language. Observing someone's body language can provide clues about their intentions. For example, someone standing very close to you may be trying to intimidate you. Or, if someone is leaning forward and making eye contact, they may be interested in what you're saying. Attention to body language can help us better understand the people around us and even improve our communication.

# What Is Positive Body Language?

## 1. Positive Facial Expressions

There's no mistaking a positive facial expression when you see one. The eyebrows are lifted, the mouth is turned up at the corners, and the eyes often crinkle at the edges. It looks like the person is about to laugh – and indeed, studies have shown that genuine smiling activates the same muscles in the face as laughter. A positive facial expression is not only a sign of happiness but also of openness and confidence. It's a way of saying, "I'm approachable, and I'm interested in what you have to say."

When we see someone exhibiting a positive facial expression – it creates a feeling of trust and rapport. We instinctively feel drawn to people who are physically open and receptive, as opposed to those who are closed off and guarded. This is why positive body language is fundamental in making first impressions: it conveys our friendliness and willingness to engage with others.

- **Smile**

A smile is the most common and universally recognized positive facial expression. It signifies happiness but can also be used to express relief, amusement, or even shyness. A genuine smile is characterized by a crinkling of the eyes, known as "Duchenne smiles," after the French physician who first described them. In contrast, a "fake smile" or "social smile" often lacks this crinkling and can be easily spotted by trained observers.

- **Nodding**

Nodding is also a positive facial expression that can signify several things. For example, nodding while someone is speaking can signal that you are listening and paying attention. Nodding can also be used to show agreement or approval, such as when you nod your head in response to a question. In some cases, nodding may also be used as a sign of respect or acknowledgment, such as when you nod to someone who has just said something noteworthy. Despite the context, nodding is generally seen as a positive gesture conveying interest, support, or agreement.

- **Laughter**

Laughter is a positive expression that signifies joy, delight, or amusement. When we laugh, our facial muscles contract and our breathing quickens. Laughter is contagious; it's often said that one cannot help but smile when one sees someone else laughing. Laughter is also good for our health; it can help to reduce stress, improve our mood, and even boost our immune system. Just a few minutes of laughter can help others feel more relaxed and happier.

Positive facial expressions don't just stop at smiles; however, facial expressions can convey a wide range of emotions, from pride and joy to compassion and love. Interestingly, many of these expressions are based on what is known as the "facial Feedback Hypothesis," which posits that our facial muscles influence our emotional state. In other words, by smiling or frowning, we can affect our emotional state. Reading and interpreting positive facial expressions and open body language can be incredibly useful in various social situations, from job interviews to first dates. By being aware of the power of nonverbal communication, we can use it to our advantage in personal and professional interactions. By sending out positive signals through our body language, we increase the chances that others will respond positively to us in turn.

### 2. Positive Eye Movements

Positive eye movement is a specific type of body language that can be particularly helpful in conveying confidence and openness. Positive eye movement involves making eye contact with the person you're talking to, as well as looking around the room and making occasional eye contact with other people in the room. This type of eye movement conveys confidence because it shows you're comfortable making eye contact and engaging with others. It also conveys openness because it shows that you're interested in what's happening around you. When combined with other forms of positive body language, positive eye movement can be a powerful tool for conveying confidence and openness.

We usually take in their body language unconsciously when we see someone. From how they carry themselves to how they interact with those around them, our brain constantly takes in these subtle cues and makes split-second decisions about the person. One of the essential cues we look for is eye movement. Where a person looks can tell us a lot about their state of mind. For example, people who are feeling guilty or shifty will often avoid eye contact. On the other hand, people who are confident and sure of themselves will usually hold your gaze.

Interestingly, eye movement can be used as a cue for positive body language. In particular, when people are around someone they find attractive, they tend to move their eyes in a "triangle" pattern, starting with the eyes, then moving to the nose, and finally to the lips. This pattern has been shown to significantly increase attraction levels, even when the participants are unaware that they are doing it! So next time you're out on a date or meeting someone new, pay attention to their eye movement. Seeing them glancing at your lips every now and then could be a good sign!

### Why Having Good Eye Contact Is Important

It's no secret that making eye contact is critical. Eye contact is essential to creating a connection, whether in a meeting, giving a presentation, or just chatting with a friend. And it's not just about making a good impression - eye contact can make you seem likable and trustworthy. But why is this?

First of all, it helps us to focus and pay attention. When making eye contact with someone, we're more likely to listen to what they're saying and less likely to be distracted by other things happening around us. Eye contact also allows us to pick up on nonverbal cues, such as facial expressions and body language, especially in negotiations or other situations where it's vital to read the other person's feelings and intentions.

Finally, making eye contact shows that we're interested in the other person and what they have to say. It sends the message that we respect them and value their opinion. So next time you're in a conversation, remember to keep your eyes on the person you're talking to - it'll make all the difference in how the conversation goes.

### 3. Positive Hand Movements

- **Firm Handshake**

A firm handshake is one of the most commonly used forms of nonverbal communication. Although a simple gesture, it can communicate a lot about a person. A firm handshake conveys confidence, trustworthiness, and professionalism. It is often used to make a good first impression in business and social settings.

The psychology behind a firm handshake is interesting. Studies have shown that people who shake hands firmly are perceived as more likable and trustworthy. This may be because a firm handshake is seen as a sign of dominance and social status. In other words, it conveys confidence and authority. When we shake someone's hand, we are essentially exchanging information about our social rank.

A firm handshake can also make you seem more competent and credible. Again, this may be because a strong grip communicates confidence and power. When shaking someone's hand, make eye contact and smile. This will help you come across as friendly and approachable.

In short, a firm handshake is a key tool for making a good first impression. It conveys confidence, trustworthiness, and competence. Next time you meet someone new, remember to shake their hand firmly.

- **Open Palms**

Open palms are a sign of positive body language. Open palms are often seen as a sign of honesty and sincerity. This is because when we open our palms, we expose our vulnerable underarms to others. This is a non-threatening gesture that shows we have nothing to hide. In contrast, closed fists or clenched hands are seen as signs of hostility or defensiveness. They communicate that we are ready to fight or defend ourselves.

The psychology behind it is that when we feel good about ourselves, we open our palms and hold them out in front of us. It's a way of displaying our confidence and showing that we're approachable. Open palms can also be a way of showing submission or pleading. For example, when we put our hands together in prayer, we're effectively saying that we're not a threat and that we're willing to listen. In a business setting, open palms can be interpreted as an offer of a handshake or an indication that we're ready to talk. They convey trustworthiness and openness, which can help build rapport. Ultimately, open palms are a sign of goodwill and positive intent, making them a crucial body language cue to be aware of.

- **Uncrossed Hands**

If you've ever seen someone with their hands clasped together in front of them, you may have wondered what it meant. Is this person praying? Meditating? Simply resting their hands? In fact, this gesture is known as the "uncrossed arms position," and it's considered to be a positive sign of body language.

There are a few possible explanations for why uncrossed arms are seen as a positive gesture. For one, it indicates that the person is relaxed and at ease. They're not tensing up or trying to hide anything, which can make them appear more trustworthy. Uncrossed arms take up less space than crossed arms, which conveys a sense of openness. This can make the person seem more approachable and inviting.

Have you ever noticed that when someone feels confident and positive, they usually keep their hands uncrossed and unfolded? There's a reason for that. Body language experts believe that crossed arms or legs are a form of self-hugging, which people do when they feel insecure or threatened. On the other hand, keeping your hands uncrossed and unfolded is a sign that you're open to what others have to say and that you're comfortable in your own skin. So next time you're in a meeting or interview for a job, make sure to keep your hands uncrossed and unfolded to send the right message.

# Positive Body Actions

### 1. Maintain Good Posture

Good posture is more than just good manners. When you stand up straight with your shoulders back, you're actually conveying a message of confidence and power. Most of us have heard that an upright and open posture is a sign of confidence, and indeed, research has shown that people with good posture are seen as more confident and competent than those who slouch. On the other hand, slouching or hunching over sends a signal of insecurity and defeat. Interestingly, research has shown that even fake confidence can lead to real success. But why is this? It turns out that our body language is closely linked to our psychological state. When we feel good about ourselves, we tend to stand up straight and open our chests, while when we feel down or defeated, we tend to slump our shoulders and close our bodies. This link between body language and inner state is so strong that it works in reverse as well: standing up straight can actually make us feel more confident, even if we don't necessarily feel it at first.

It's not just about looking good, though. Maintaining an upright posture has many physical benefits. It helps to keep your spine in alignment, which prevents pain and improves your overall mobility. Also, good posture helps you breathe more easily and deeply, increasing your energy levels and concentration. In short, there are a few problems that can't be helped by simply standing up straight. So, the next time you find yourself slouching, take a moment to correct your posture. Not only will you look more confident, but you'll also be doing your body a favor.

## 2. Lean in While Talking or Listening

Good communication is essential to any successful relationship, whether professional or personal. One of the critical elements of effective communication is body language. The way we carry ourselves and interact with others can say a lot about what we're thinking and feeling, even if we're not saying anything. One common form of body language is leaning in. When we see someone leaning in while listening to us speak, it generally gives the impression that this person is interested in what we have to say. They are making themselves available to us and are sending the message that they want to hear what we have to say. It's a nonverbal way of saying "I'm listening," and it helps to create a rapport between speaker and listener. In contrast, leaning away from someone can signal disinterest or impatience.

Some studies suggest that leaning in while speaking can make the conversation feel more enjoyable for both parties. When we lean in while speaking, it signals to the other person that we are engaged and invested in the conversation. This can make them feel more comfortable and lead to a more positive interaction overall. Our body language can send many different signals, but leaning in is definitely one of the most positive. It shows interest, engagement, and respect for the other person and can help to make any conversation more enjoyable, so if you want to show that you care about what someone is saying, lean in and make eye contact. It might just make all the difference in the world.

# Chapter 4: How to Gain Confidence and Get Respect

Confidence is not a skill; it is a way of thinking that evolves. Positive thinking, regular practice, formal training, increased knowledge, and social interaction can all help you build up your confidence.

Gaining self-confidence is the first step toward being socially successful.
*https://unsplash.com/photos/hQP5mWcM84c*

Feeling good about yourself, appreciating your physical and mental abilities, and having faith in your knowledge and experience are all necessary ingredients for a healthy dose of confidence. Most people want to feel more confident, and it is possible to do so.

This chapter is about helping you gain and boost your confidence and appreciate the worth of others.

## What Is Self-Confidence?

Although many people have different definitions for self-confidence, it essentially means believing in oneself. Your confidence level is influenced by what you have been through and how you learned to deal with adversity. Your self-esteem fluctuates over time.

A person's level of self-assurance usually reflects the values and lessons they have learned throughout their lives.

How we are taught to see and act shapes our core assumptions about who we are and how we should treat others. This has also been influenced by environmental factors we have experienced, be they an abusive childhood or a happy, well-balanced upbringing. Our confidence in our ability to handle our responsibilities and deal with difficult situations varies from person to person.

### Low-Confidence

Apprehension about the future, negative feedback, dissatisfaction with one's appearance, failure to plan ahead or to acquire the necessary skills, and an inability to learn from mistakes can all lead to a lack of confidence.

When you lack confidence in yourself, it is usually because you are concerned about what other people think of you. This type of thinking may prevent you from doing what you know is beneficial for you out of fear of discomfort or embarrassment.

### Over-Confidence

An unhealthy dose of confidence can lead to the false belief that any goal can be achieved, even if the individual lacks the necessary competence. In these circumstances, misplaced confidence frequently backfires.

An overinflated sense of self-assurance increases the likelihood that others will perceive you as conceited or arrogant. People are more likely to rejoice in your downfall if they see you as arrogant and insufferable.

However, you don't want this; you want to demonstrate a healthy amount of confidence that will garner the respect of others.

## Is Confidence Necessary for Good Health?

When you have a positive self-image, it'll show in the decisions you make. Your chances of improving aspects of your lifestyle, such as self-care, social engagement, physical activity, and diet, increase.

Positivity and an optimistic outlook on life also benefit your mental and emotional health and stem from self-assurance. If you lack confidence, your sense of self-worth and dignity may suffer.

When you lack confidence, making decisions and confronting problems can be difficult. You could begin to doubt your abilities. Meeting new people and joining in new activities could become very challenging.

You might withdraw and avoid social situations for fear of offending others. All these things could result in a negative spiral as you begin avoiding situations that make you feel uneasy, further eroding your confidence.

## Respect and Its Meanings

Respect is one of the fundamental cornerstones of successful interpersonal relationships and one's sense of self. Respect is a basic universal need. It plays a significant role in shaping who we are as individuals and strengthening our bonds with one another.

Tolerating another individual is an attempt to avoid treating them rudely. It's a concept that suggests we should respect someone else's words and actions even if we don't always agree with or support them. When you respect someone, you do not pass judgment on them based on their ideas, actions, or beliefs.

### Why Is It Important to Show Respect?

If we don't value ourselves, no one else will. Having a safe space where people can express themselves without fear of being judged is critical.

When you respect yourself and others, it inevitably shows in your interactions with them and with the rest of the world. Your interactions with others become increasingly respectful and harmonious over time.

Respecting yourself and others allows you to form deeper relationships. Respectful behavior enhances your ability to establish and maintain meaningful relationships with other people, regardless of the setting.

When you take care of yourself, value yourself, and appreciate others, you become more secure, happier, and more prosperous.

## Instances of Respectful Behavior

Below are some illustrative instances of respect:

### Listening

Everyone needs attention and acknowledgment. Listening to what someone has to say is a basic form of courtesy. You shouldn't even consider whether they have anything worthwhile to contribute or not. When you spend time with another individual, you demonstrate respect for them.

### Supporting

Giving someone your support shows them that you believe in them and their ability to make a difference. You can make others feel important and worthy of respect. Sharing a virtual badge of support can be a simple way to show your admiration for someone. Simply observing and expressing something positive about someone will show your support.

### Practicing Kindness

Kindness is distinct from service to someone. Compassion doesn't require someone "deserving" it, but it's difficult to feel compassion if you don't believe it's deserved. When you show kindness to others, you demonstrate selflessness and generosity. Kindness is fundamentally a sign of respect; being respectful and assisting those in need are inextricably linked.

### Being Courteous

Treating someone courteously is one of the simplest ways to gain respect. A pleasant demeanor can make people feel valued and happy. To keep your hard-won respect, you must be polite to yourself and others.

# Importance of Confidence in Social Interactions

Being self-assured also has numerous benefits for your social relationships. Consider the following benefits of confidence:

### You Are Free to Be Yourself

Being yourself among a group of people will be much easier if you have a healthy dose of confidence and self-respect. People can usually tell when you're being genuine. When you feel safe enough to express your true self, the likelihood of having a meaningful conversation with another person increases.

### Capacity to Express Yourself

When you have a healthy sense of self-worth, you are more likely to stand up for what you believe in and to persevere in the face of adversity. This strength helps you to maintain your integrity and authenticity even when confronted by an opponent. When you are confident, you will be free of the anxiety that comes with self-doubt.

### Take Pride in Yourself and Your Abilities

A solid sense of self-confidence also allows you to appreciate who you are and what you are capable of to a greater extent. Similar to the preceding advantage, this will result in stronger relationships with others and an improved outlook on life. Additionally, it will facilitate more enjoyable and productive social connections.

### Improved Performance

Self-confidence boosts performance. Instead of wasting time and resources fretting about your inadequacy, you could focus your efforts.

### Better Connections

Self-assurance influences your outlook on life and your ability to understand and appreciate those around you. It strengthens your resolve to leave a partner who doesn't meet your expectations.

### Willingness to Try New Things

When you believe in yourself, you are more open to new experiences. Taking risks, such as applying for a new job or enrolling in a culinary class, becomes much easier when you have self-confidence.

# Techniques for Boosting Confidence and Social Standing

There are two parts to developing self-confidence. While it is important to work on improving your internal sense of self-assurance, it is equally necessary to think about how you project an outward sense of assurance and win the admiration of others. The list below contains several potential strategies for accomplishing this.

### Get Involved with Upbeat Individuals

Consider the emotional impact your friends have on you for a moment. Do they make you feel good or bad? Do you feel constantly judged, or are you eventually accepted?

Your friends can influence your self-esteem more than you realize. Consequently, you should be aware of the feelings of those around you. If being around someone makes you feel bad about yourself, don't be afraid to cut ties with them.

Instead, surround yourself with people who genuinely care about your success. Surrounding yourself with positive, supportive people can boost your confidence, overall well-being, and outlook. Self-assurance and a positive attitude go hand in hand.

### Take Better Care of Your Body

One way to increase your self-esteem is to stop harming your body, which only makes you feel bad about yourself. As much as it is a buzzword these days, self-care is a fundamental factor in balancing your overall health. By caring for yourself, you improve your emotional, mental, and physical health, which in turn increases your self-esteem.

You can boost your confidence by engaging in the following self-care routines:

### Diet

A healthy diet has several advantages, including increased self-worth and self-confidence. Consuming nutrient-dense meals improves your health, strength, and energy levels, all of which can boost your self-esteem.

### Exercise

Self-esteem increases as body image improves. Physical activity is an easy way to boost one's self-esteem; the more you do it, the better you'll feel.

### Meditation

Meditation is a pleasant way to unwind and has several advantages for one's self-esteem. The quiet time can be used for introspection, so you recognize and accept yourself. Meditation may also help you learn to silence the dissenting voice in your head and disengage from the stream of meaningless thoughts that may diminish your confidence.

### Sleep

Sleep deprivation will have a negative impact on your mood. Conversely, adequate sleep is associated with more optimistic traits such as enthusiasm and happiness. Self-care is critical for self-esteem.

### Confront Your Fears

Don't put off dating or job hunting because you're insecure. Facing and overcoming your fears can help you feel more confident in these situations.

Recognize and name some of the fears that have prevented you from reaching your full potential. Even if you are afraid of humiliating yourself or making a mistake, you should try anyway. Having doubts could work in your favor and even help you perform better. Convince yourself that it is only a test, and then observe the results.

Perhaps you will realize that your fears were unfounded or that making a few mistakes is not the end of the world and the cherry on top is that your self-esteem will grow as you progress. Ultimately, fear could prevent you from making decisions with far-reaching, possibly catastrophic consequences.

### Do What You're Best At

What happens when you focus on your strengths? Your self-esteem begins to rise. When you concentrate on your strengths, they become even more powerful, and your confidence grows. A secondary benefit of putting this strategy in place is increased life satisfaction.

There is a link between self-efficacy (the belief that you can improve on your strengths) and happiness. And to strengthen this link, begin with recognizing your strengths.

If you're skilled at your chosen sport, make it a priority to play or practice it once or twice per week. Focus on doing those things you're good at more often in the workplace. Developing your skills will help you gain self-confidence.

**Master the Art of Saying No**

Confidence can be boosted by participating in activities in which you excel, but it's also necessary to be aware of situations that undermine it. Perhaps you've noticed that a certain hobby always makes you feel bad about yourself.

You have the right to decline an invitation or participate in activities that could lower your self-esteem. You should be aware, however, that experiencing pain is a normal part of learning new skills and broadening your horizons; therefore, don't avoid activities that have this effect altogether. While pushing your limits is beneficial, understanding your limits is essential, so work towards finding a happy medium.

Establishing healthy limits for your emotional and social sharing will increase your sense of mental security. It also gives you a sense of control. Being in control of your life is a key component of self-confidence. Boundaries contribute to this sense of control.

If someone else suggests something that makes you uncomfortable, politely decline. Similarly, you do not have to avoid it altogether. After figuring out how to improve your self-assurance, you will feel ready to give it another shot.

**Set Attainable Goals**

When pursuing one's goals, part and parcel of reaching them is that you will probably fail several times before discovering a strategy that works. This may cause you to doubt your own abilities. When this happens, you may wonder how to boost your confidence without jeopardizing your goals. The answer is to set realistic goals at work towards them in small steps.

Setting lofty goals and failing to meet them will lower your confidence. In contrast, realistic goals are attainable. The more successful you are, the more confident you will be in your own abilities and significance, and the bigger your goals can become.

Putting your goals in writing is a great way to ensure they don't get lost or forgotten. Afterward, evaluate your chances of success. The goal may be too lofty if your chances of success are slim. Reduce it to make it more feasible and workable.

### Embrace Self-Compassion

One way to practice self-compassion is to be gentle with yourself when you make mistakes or fall short of your goals. You'll be able to connect with yourself and others more deeply as you learn to be flexible with your emotions and deal with the difficult ones.

There is a link between self-compassion and self-assurance. Knowing that failure or flaws are normal and expected makes dealing with adversity easier the next time it occurs. Try to treat yourself with compassion as you endure this difficulty.

### Use Healthy Self-Talk

When you tell yourself, "I can't stand this," or "this is too difficult," or "I shouldn't even try," you're telling your mind that you can't do it and that your abilities are inadequate. Positive self-talk can help you better understand yourself, boosting your confidence and allowing you to take on larger tasks.

When you start to feel like you don't belong in a meeting, remind yourself that negative ideas aren't always correct. The next step is to learn how to replace negative self-talk with constructive alternatives.

Consider the following suggestions to boost your self-esteem by combating negative self-talk:

"I am not strong enough" or "I cannot accomplish this" becomes "I have nothing to lose by trying" or "I have everything to gain by succeeding."

The negative self-talk of "I can't do it right" is replaced by positive self-talk such as "I will do better" or "I learned something."

### Develop Your Assertiveness

When you are assertive, you value and advocate for the needs and perspectives of others while also acquiring the same for yourself.

One technique is to observe aggressive people and mimic their actions to a certain degree.

You shouldn't pretend to be someone else, though. Instead, it is about taking cues from people you admire and allowing your authentic self to shine through.

# 50 Simple Ways to Gain Respect While Staying Confident

Everyone wants respect, whether from a superior, peer, or loved one. Earning that respect, however, takes work. You must first learn to respect others before you can expect to be trusted.

Here is a comprehensive list of simple yet effective methods for gaining respect:

1. Be more giving than receiving Respect must be given before it can be received.
2. Have self-respect: True respect begins from within.
3. Show respect: Respect your surroundings.
4. Maintain your integrity: Honesty is the foundation upon which respect is built.
5. Keep your word: Only those who keep their promises are respected.
6. Add value: Your reputation will improve as you become more concerned about the well-being of others.
7. Resist the urge to reveal everything that comes to mind: Nobody needs to know what you're thinking. To earn respect, keep things simple.
8. Consider the feelings of others: They are as important as you are.
9. Adhere to the facts: Explain yourself truthfully.
10. Pay attention to the things that truly matter: Spend your time and energy on important things.
11. Step out of your comfort zone: People admire those who take risks and seek new challenges.
12. Set aside your judgment: Expect to be criticized, but don't judge others.
13. Put your ideals into action: Don't just talk about your values; put them into action.
14. Be genuine: Don't be afraid to take risks, do things your own way in life and be true to yourself.

15. Express gratitude: The most admired individuals express their gratitude with clarity and positivity.
16. Be truthful while remaining diplomatic: It's better to be honest than impressive.
17. Maintain a positive attitude: People value optimism.
18. Make every effort to influence major issues: Those who recognize which fights are worthwhile are admired.
19. Be inquisitive: Ask open-ended questions and pay attention.
20. Make an extra effort: Bring others with you. Outperform all expectations.
21. Create connections: Associate with individuals who share your values.
22. Understand your priorities: Determine the most important aspects of your life so that you can prioritize them.
23. Leverage your likeability: No matter your title, you can still work to develop meaningful relationships with your colleagues.
24. You should have an excellent memory: Inquiring about a person's significant life events may elicit strong positive reactions.
25. Abdicate responsibility when appropriate: If you allow others to demonstrate their power and admire them for it, they will return the favor and respect you more.
26. Be motivating: People who inspire others to greatness are generally the most respected.
27. Always be punctual: It shows consideration for others.
28. Consider the future: Consider other people and try to figure out how you can help them get answers or make changes that will benefit them.
29. Express yourself: Respect is earned by having strong opinions and many ideas. Just don't make a big deal out of it.
30. Get yourself ready: Understanding what to expect from each engagement, meeting, or discussion demonstrates respect.
31. Do not be afraid to ask how you can help. Do not avoid people who are in pain. Even if they decline your offer, you

will leave a lasting impression.
32. Own it: Be confident in your abilities without being arrogant, and be proud of what you've accomplished without trying to hide it.
33. Respect the dignity of others: This fundamental approach is invaluable.
34. Apologize: If you make a mistake, simply apologize.
35. Trust your instincts: It is critical to recognize when something feels wrong.
36. Don't get too worked up over trivial details: Again, these are minor details.
37. Understand how to say no: Respect grows when one can confidently say "no" and explain why.
38. Follow a moral code: Determine your values and demonstrate them to the rest of the world through small acts of kindness and honesty.
39. Never fail to meet a deadline: The best way to show respect is to complete tasks efficiently and on time.
40. Recognize the worth of individuals who are difficult to value: Respecting someone's behavior isn't always necessary, but respecting the person is.
41. Hear various points of view: Listen carefully to others and value different points of view.
42. Be willing to make concessions: Collaborate with others to find a solution that appeals to everyone.
43. You should not kiss and tell: It's often the words you don't say that matter most.
44. Choose your fights wisely: There are times when you must compromise your values to maintain harmony.
45. Choose the high path: Set challenging but achievable daily goals for yourself, and push yourself to meet them.
46. Practice genuine listening: Listening intently demonstrates concern.
47. Never squander anyone's time: Recognize the significance of people's free time.

48. Accept responsibility: Take full responsibility for everything you do, both personally and professionally.
49. Put on good clothes: People form impressions in a matter of seconds.
50. Understand your triggers: Be aware of what triggers your emotions and avoid getting carried away.

The first step toward living a meaningful life is developing the confidence and self-assurance necessary to relate to others effectively, alongside the skills required to establish meaningful relationships.

# Chapter 5: Increase Your Charisma and Start Turning Heads!

Charisma is a personality trait that many people believe is innate. However, some people are born with it, while others are not. Researchers have confirmed that charisma, like any other personality trait, can be learned and developed by anyone who wishes to do so for themselves. Some people are more charismatic than others because they are more intentional about developing their charisma. They have demonstrated consistency over time to the point where it has become a part of them. Given that you can cultivate charisma think about how you might do it for yourself.

Charismatic people know how to turn heads.
*https://unsplash.com/photos/RNiBLy7aHck*

However, before we get there, consider the following reasons for increasing your charisma:

## Importance of Increasing Your Charisma

The following are some advantages to having and developing charisma.

### More People Will Like You

You'll attract more people who will support and encourage you daily. Increasing your charisma makes people like you more. People notice your confidence in what you do, your enthusiasm and courage in your dealings, and want to be associated with you. All of this is possible because you have worked on developing your charisma to the point where it is noticeable.

### You Can Rally Support Easily

You don't need to cut corners in your interpersonal relationships if you have good charisma. You can effectively present yourself authentically and persuade people to support and stand with you through your words, actions, and body language.

### People Will Be Committed to Your Cause

Charisma benefits your interpersonal relationships because you'll be able to keep your relationships with people longer. People who observe your charisma have confidence in your personality and your understanding of their uniqueness. This uniqueness keeps them close because it is lovely to find someone who understands you and with whom you feel at ease. For your sake, these people remain committed to your cause and even become advocates for it. This commitment creates a circle of people who are loyal and committed to you.

### You Will Have a Better Chance at Success

When you surround yourself with quality people because of your charisma, you'll achieve more and be happier. Building quality relationships around yourself allow you to leverage the strengths, time, and competence of others more easily than you would otherwise. You discover that you are never alone because people are always willing to assist you.

Given the significance of increasing your charisma, how can you do it? In the next section, you'll learn the secrets to developing your charisma and reaping the rewards that come with it.

## How to Increase Your Charisma

We've established that charisma is a character trait that, if desired, can be learned and developed. Here are some tips for increasing your charisma and attracting people's attention.

### Stay Focused

Increasing your charisma will mean remaining focused on the task at hand. Whether it's a conversation with an individual, a presentation before a board of directors, a business pitch, or a lecture to an audience, you must remain focused and avoid distractions.

Focusing on the present moment will help you keep track of your words and actions, giving your audience the impression that you know what you're talking about. Whether on a date or having a casual conversation with a friend, you must show your companion that you're giving them your full attention.

A small act of kindness like this makes them feel like they belong in your company and comfortable enough to open up to you about things they wouldn't have otherwise. People will lose interest in being around you if you don't exhibit this trait. When you do not pay complete attention to someone or a group of people, they will notice because you will lose track of the conversation at some point and force them to repeat themselves.

One method for staying focused is to ask questions that require the person to give a deeper explanation of some points than others. For starters, it shows that you are with them mentally and emotionally and allows them to communicate clearly with you, leaving nothing for you to assume.

### Spread Warmth

Charismatic people are generally considered friendly and accessible. Warmth in communication increases people's likelihood of trusting and following your views.

The effectiveness of a sincere smile is often underestimated, yet it may go a long way toward spreading positivity. Smiling at someone gives off the impression that you are kind and optimistic, two qualities essential to charm. Mirror neurons in the nervous system are turned on when someone smiles, which makes the other person smile back.

### Express Passion

One of the most appealing aspects of charisma is its infectious enthusiasm. Charismatic individuals are enthusiastic and energetic. Other people feel compelled to take action just by being in their presence.

People are sensitive to others' feelings. Powerful emotions spread like wildfire. So, if you work with someone who is often feeling down at work, your mood will also go down if you're not careful. Similarly, you might feel the same way if you're talking to someone enthusiastic and upbeat.

### Be Smart

Smartness is seen in how you put yourself together - your clothing, appearance, demeanor, approach to issues, mannerisms, and gestures. Being smart is about both physical appearance and intellectual expression. If you look after yourself, you will feel good about yourself, and that will show in how others treat you.

Smartness stems, first and foremost, from self-assurance. If you want to look smart, you should always have a pleasant expression and never show signs of strain on your face. Your audience will have no interest in your worries, nor will they care particularly, so stay cheerful, and you'll end up with more people who have your back and will support you simply because you are charismatic.

You believe in yourself and your abilities, and your demeanor reflects this. Smart people are always open to knowledge and learning, which allows them to continue on the path of self-development indefinitely.

### Listen Attentively

To *actively listen* means to process what the other person is saying in real-time, to follow along with the conversation naturally, to note the other person's questions, and to make mental notes about what they are observing.

An active listener observes the speaker's body language, an essential aspect of any conversation. Being attentive also implies that you are not simply listening, so you can respond as fast as possible and often defensively. Instead of waiting for the other person to finish talking so you can start dishing out your arguments, react to what they said, acknowledge it, and engage with them.

It is critical to assure your speaker that you have no preconceived notions about what they are saying. This act boosts both your own and the speaker's confidence.

**Learn Storytelling**

Storytelling makes public speaking and participation more enjoyable and interesting. It connects your listeners to you as you speak, whether they are a large audience, a small group of people, or just one person. Including stories in your speech helps to keep it interesting. If you want to help your audience better understand your message and lighten a serious moment in your public engagements, don't be afraid to draw on personal experiences, whether your own or those of others.

Think of ways to draw parallels between what you're talking about and events happening now or that have occurred in the past. If you can't think of any, make up some fictional stories to support your point and help your audience understand you better.

If you want to convey your point effectively, use real-life examples. These real-life examples allow your audience to check your claims and see what might happen in similar situations.

**Be Audience Specific**

Be flexible in your communication and relationships. You must know what works in your communication and relationships with specific individuals or groups. Your principles should be firm and stern, but your application should be flexible because different people or groups will require a different approach in your interactions with them. You will be more specific and direct in your dealings with people if you learn to apply different strategies in your communication and relationships with diverse audiences. This flexibility boosts your confidence and, in turn, your charisma.

Another advantage is that you'll learn not to speak over your audience. It's also imperative you talk to your audience in the type of language they understand. The language you use with students should be different from the language you use with adults in business. Learn to use the words and actions that best convey your message to each audience. This language flexibility will help to improve communication and interpersonal relationships.

## Be Observant

Your ability to read beyond what people say is a skill that will help you increase your charisma. Pay attention to their emotions and body language as you relate to or communicate with others. You can read between the lines of their actions and gestures, which is often as informative as the words they use.

To boost your charisma, you must learn to be highly observant. Observe people's attitudes, temperaments, emotions, and gestures as you communicate. When you use this trait, you'll boost your own sense of self-worth and theirs. If you work on this trait, you'll be able to understand people even when they can't talk to you or tell you what's bothering them.

On the other hand, you must master your body language and use it appropriately in your relationships and interactions with others. When you use your body language correctly, you can send the same message with your words and actions without contradicting each other.

Keep your communication and body language consistent to avoid sowing any seed of distrust in the hearts of those around you. Ensure your words and actions are in sync while communicating.

Maintain an air of confidence at all times. People admire you when you are confident in yourself because that is a quality many desire.

## Always Remember

People appreciate it when you recall previous interactions and bring them up in subsequent meetings. This simple act of recollection boosts your charisma by demonstrating how much you value your interactions with them, especially the positive ones. It is also a tool that gets you more respect than many others. This is why you should prioritize remembering people's names, kind gestures, loyalty, encouragement, and support. It may also be necessary to refer to these things occasionally to express appreciation for the individual.

People enjoy being appreciated, and a grateful heart attracts more favors. Similarly, people appreciate it when you remember their names the next time you see them. It makes them feel loved and wanted and shows them that you value their presence.

These are the kinds of thoughtful gestures that help build strong relationships, which in turn boost your charisma.

### Stop Complaining

Everyone goes through tough times, but it's the one who brings them to light who's labeled as negative. When you meet new people, try to keep your worries and concerns under wraps as much as possible. It is not a charismatic trait to be known for always having complaints. This incessant complaint will negatively impact your confidence, and people will avoid you.

You may have some close friends with whom you can discuss your concerns and develop creative solutions. Make every effort to keep them within that circle and no further. Do not constantly bombard people with your worries; this will wear them down and cause you to lose their respect. Instead, consider solutions to the problems and show people your worth rather than your flaws.

### Keep Your Head Up

This act should have been first on our list, but it may sound like a cliche, so we decided to bring it up now. Yes, keeping your head up while walking down the street, talking to a stranger, giving a presentation, or speaking in front of an audience is a noble act. It is the first sign of a self-assured person, making others respect you.

Holding your head up high allows you to maintain eye contact with people while communicating with them. It is a valuable skill. Maintaining eye contact with people demonstrates your confidence, which tells the person you're dealing with that they can also trust you.

It is easy to persuade people to accept what you bring to the table if they see that you are confident in your words, and many unpleasant issues can be acceptable if presented correctly. This is part of the unspoken part of the conversation, and you will do well to notice it in others as you interact with them. This act may be hard at first, but if you keep doing it, you will learn it and be able to do it more often.

### Compliment Genuinely

Practice freely and sincerely complimenting others. This simple act may appear insignificant, but it dramatically increases your charisma. Compliments should be given with enthusiasm, as they boost the self-esteem of those with whom you are conversing.

Compliments have a way of lifting people's spirits. For example, someone walks up to you, unsure of how they look, most likely due to some issues they have, and you tell them right away how beautiful or handsome they are or how beautifully dressed they are.

The first thing you should expect from such a person is a smile, and you should be able to get them to relax their nerves and worry less about whatever it was they had to deal with. Genuine compliments demonstrate to others how much attention you pay to details about them.

Talk about their moods, clothes, nice perfumes, makeup, and facial expressions. When people know you notice these things, they will be eager to hear your thoughts whenever they contact you. This act makes you more confident, which increases your charisma.

Increasing your charisma will get you into the right circles faster than you would otherwise. As this chapter discusses, you must learn and start practicing the skill. Since it's not a genetic predisposition, you can train yourself to become more affable as soon as you like and benefit from it in your social interactions. To accomplish this, you should always show that you are present to the person(s) in front of you by paying close attention to them. Focus on the topic and avoid distractions from others or your devices like phones or computers. For the sake of concentration, you should turn them off or put them on silent. Make yourself comfortable and show it during every conversation. People tend to relax when they see how relaxed and comfortable you are, which makes for more confidence in each other as you communicate. As the conversation progresses, demonstrate that you are paying attention by repeating what the person has said at intervals. Ask relevant questions that allow them to clarify, occasionally nodding your head, and use as much body language as possible to let them know you are fully engaged in the conversation. Learn to listen to people's words rather than just responding to them. To be a good listener, you must be able to empathetically put yourself in the speaker's shoes and evaluate their words without any preconceived notions or prejudices. When it is your turn to speak, try to pause for a few moments before doing so. That will give you time to gather your thoughts before responding.

Always exude confidence by moving or speaking with your head held high. Be smart at all times, and let people see your enthusiasm. Maintain occasional eye contact and always wear a smile. Learn to freely and sincerely compliment others. People want to know that you genuinely care about their well-being, which you can demonstrate by observing them beyond what they say.

There is a lot to learn about a person, from their facial expressions, gestures while speaking, attitude, and even how they express their emotions. While looking for these signs, make your body language match what you're saying. Instilling faith in your audience will encourage them to commit fully to you and your cause. When you have the opportunity to meet people again, remember and call them by their names, remind them of previous conversations, or notice something striking about them that you noticed when you first met. This makes them feel valued and appreciated on your part. Find out how to lighten the mood with a few well-timed jokes and a good story.

Learning what works best for each individual or group is crucial when communicating with others. Don't use the same strategy for everyone you meet because it may not always work. In addition, learn not to burden others with grumbling. For one thing, they may be unable to assist you and may avoid you. Constantly complaining makes you appear unhappy, which harms your charisma. Do your best to be a valuable person rather than someone known for complaining. Take your time studying these and putting them into practice. They may be difficult initially, but the more you practice, the easier they will become, and the better you'll get on with people.

# Chapter 6: 14 Psychological Tricks to Influence People

Are you having trouble getting people to do what you want? Do you feel like everyone is resistant to your ideas and suggestions? Sometimes it feels like the best way for us to get others to listen to us or do what we want is by tricking them. What if you knew some tricks would make it easier for us to get what we want from others? It turns out there are, but not in the ways you might think.

The world of advertising, branding, and marketing uses subtle techniques to persuade people to buy a product or service. These psychological tricks are used to influence people by appealing to basic instincts and human behavior. They bypass logical defenses and take advantage of universal flaws in human nature, such as irrational fears, a love of novelty, and the tendency to follow social norms.

There are several tips and tricks to help you get people's attention.
*https://unsplash.com/photos/LQ1t-8Ms5PY*

It sounds unethical and sneaky, and sometimes it is. But in reality, many useful psychological tricks positively influence people. You, too, can learn these techniques (ethically) when you need to get someone on your side. This chapter covers 14 different ways you can use psychology to influence other people for the better while also looking into how psychological trickery actually works. These are not manipulation techniques – but they are strategies anyone can use at home or work with excellent results.

## What Are Psychological Tricks?

Psychological tricks are a collection of techniques that can be used to influence a person's thoughts, feelings, or behavior. They can be used in various situations, such as to influence the actions of others or to change your own behavior and thinking. They come in many different forms too. Some involve using social influence, such as influencing people by using power, authority, or popularity. Other tricks rely on cognitive biases, such as anchoring and social proof.

Psychological tricks can be used for good or for sinister purposes. They can be used by those who want to do good things, such as by encouraging positive behavior or helping people overcome adversity. But they can also be used by others who might want to do bad things, such as by manipulating people into doing something they don't want to do or by causing them to make a poor decision that leads to negative consequences.

If you use psychological tricks, it's essential to think carefully about what you're trying to achieve and how your actions might affect others. You should also be aware that there is no one-size-fits-all solution to influencing others – each situation is different, so you must tailor your approach accordingly.

## How Can Psychological Tricks Make People Like Me?

When you first meet a person, there are certain things you're looking for. Things like how they look and if they seem interesting or likable. In the same way, we're all looking to see how people feel about us. This is where the idea of "likeability" comes in. People want to be liked by others because it makes them feel good and helps them fit in.

And the way to be liked is to act like you're easy to get along with and show positive emotions such as joy, happiness, excitement, and intelligence. So what can you do to make yourself more "likable?" Well, psychological tricks can help you determine what you need to do in each situation, more specifically, how you should act. For example, smile more often and use your body language to make yourself more approachable. Or show your true emotions – this will help people trust you more and like you faster!

# 14 Psychological Tricks to Influence People

Knowing psychological tricks to influence people is a good idea because it can help you to be more persuasive when trying to get someone to do what you want or to like you. This kind of knowledge can also help you avoid making bad decisions that could have serious consequences. There are many different kinds of psychological tricks, and knowing them all is not possible. However, you can get a better understanding of the main ones. This will help you know what to look for when dealing with others. By knowing the main types of psychological tricks, you can take control of the situation and limit its impact on your life.

### 1. Build Trust before Making Your Request

If you don't have trust, people are less likely to comply with your requests.

- One way to build trust is by giving a gift or a favor. A gift can be something as small as a cup of coffee or a pen. Giving a gift shows that you're trustworthy and that you care
- Another way to build trust is by using a legitimate authority. An example is when someone goes to the doctor and asks for advice. The doctor's title and profession build trust
- Another way to build trust is by using the right language. If you want to persuade someone, use the person's name and make sure you address them as "you."

### 2. Use the Foot-in-the-Door Technique

With this technique, you ask for a small commitment from people before asking for a more considerable commitment. For example, if you're trying to sell something, ask for a small commitment first, like asking for the person's email address. After you get a small commitment, you can ask for a more significant commitment. However, before you make that request, you have to give something in return. You have to make the person feel like they've received value from their commitment. If you want to get people to donate to a cause, make them sign up for a newsletter or a mailing list. If you want people to vote for someone, get them to put a sticker on their car or wear a t-shirt first.

### 3. Use Reciprocity to Build Agreement

Reciprocity is the rule that people feel an obligation to return a favor. If you want someone to agree with your statement or with your request, give them something first. The most common way to apply this technique is to give people a gift before asking them to do something. An example is when you're at a trade convention. You approach a person and ask them to try your product. The person declines your offer. You can give that person a gift, such as a pen or a key chain. After the gift exchange, you can ask the person to try your product. Sometimes, you have to give something to get something.

### 4. Leverage the Power of Language and Words

To persuade someone, you have to use language that affects the person's emotions. The most powerful words are the ones that evoke strong emotions. These words include words like "free," "new," "win," "easy," "latest," and "exciting." If you want to persuade someone, you must use words that evoke positive emotions. If you have to write a persuasive essay, you have to use persuasive words and phrases. You have to go beyond the basic words and use words that have *compelling power*.

### 5. Treat Other People How They Want to Be Treated

The self-verification theory is the idea that people are more likely to gravitate toward others who have the same subconscious feeling about them as they do themselves.

It explains why people unconsciously choose to confirm their beliefs and stick with their existing views and opinions, no matter how much evidence contradicts those views and opinions.

For example, suppose you believe that everyone should recycle. In that case, you're more likely to look for evidence of recycling in the environment than someone who doesn't recycle. We are selectively seeking out information confirming our beliefs while ignoring contradictory evidence.

This theory also states that individuals seek information from others who validate their beliefs and perceptions. For example, suppose an individual believes they are intelligent. In that case, they will seek out information or another person who confirms this belief and avoid information that suggests they are not. An article published in 2121 in the University of California Press suggests that self-verification works because we are more likely to trust someone who acts the same way as we do.

### 6. Create Shared Values

Emphasizing shared values is not just a nice way to say, "we're alike." A lack of shared values, or at least a strong disagreement in values, can be an obstacle to influencing other people to like you. And poor relationships are one of the biggest reasons people fail to get what they want from someone else. Research published in the National Library of Medicine suggests that shared values are integral to guiding behavior because they create bonding. But people with different values won't agree on how to achieve common goals. They can even have conflicting goals. And if this happens often enough, it can create a toxic relationship that drains time and energy without leading to any progress.

To create similar values, you can start by assessing what other people believe in and making a stand about what they value most. Then, ask them how you can help them pursue those same values. When people share their values, it makes them more likely to listen and accept new ideas from others. And when they do this, they begin to build trust and respect for each other.

### 7. Leaders Are Warm and Competent

As the Harvard Business Review highlighted, corporations' and CEO-specific training programs suggest warmth and competence help gain subordinates' trust. When people are friendly and approachable, they make people feel comfortable. People trust them, and they want to follow them.

Common attributes of these characteristics include:

- Building trust by being genuine and authentic
- Being clear about what they want, and they make sure everyone knows the goals and expectations

- Being honest and open, always looking for ways to improve things
- Being decisive and making decisions without hesitation while also being able to adapt to changing situations as they arise
- Having an abundance of empathy, understanding how other people feel, and thinking about how their decisions will impact others
- They are visionary, always looking ahead at what needs to be done next, anticipating future challenges, and finding ways to overcome them

## 8. Be Kind to Others by Complimenting Them

Spontaneous trait transference (STT) refers to the transmission of an individual's character traits from one person to another. It is a form of social influence in that it can occur between individuals who are close in some way, such as family members or friends. STT has been observed in many circumstances, including adoption, shared living situations, and joint schooling. Individuals with strong interpersonal skills are more likely to exhibit STT, which suggests that it might be related to empathy. A study conducted by researchers in the National Library of Medicine looking into the phenomenon of spontaneous trait transference confirmed that spontaneous trait transference is the unconscious tendency for a person to express their feelings and attitudes in the same manner as certain other people they know. In other words, it is when someone unconsciously takes on the traits of someone else.

To put this in the perspective of influencing other people. When you use positive language with someone, those same positive traits will be seen in you by other people. For example, if you compliment someone, they will transfer that same positivity to you, thereby making them feel like you are worthy of the same compliments.

## 9. Be Around the Person More Often

An academic theory suggests frequent contact with an object, person, activity, or sound can lead individuals to consider the stimulus as a more appealing one. This is known as the mere-exposure effect, outlined in BMC Psychology. The *mere-exposure effect* is a psychological phenomenon that refers to the tendency for people to like things more after they've seen them more often. The mere exposure effect can be seen in a number of different domains, including advertising and music. For example, in music, people's favorite songs often become more popular after their favorite artists perform them on TV shows or radio.

Spending more time with someone can lead to liking that person. It's not surprising, really. After all, we're social animals, and spending time with others is one of the key ways that we can increase our chances of survival. As a result, when we spend more time with someone, they'll likely develop a stronger sense of familiarity and comfort around us. This can eventually lead to feelings of liking in return. One way to increase the chances of this happening is to make an effort to spend time with people on a regular basis. You don't have to go out for drinks every night — just make sure you spend some time with other people each day.

### 10. Display Positive Emotions

Positive emotions are attractive, and they can make you more likable. Things like joy, excitement, happiness, and enthusiasm are all positive emotions. When you're feeling them, it shows in your body language. For example, if you smile when you're talking to someone, the other person will likely feel that you're happy and friendly. Feeling positive emotions also makes you more likely to be optimistic about the future. This optimism can help you approach life with a sense of joy and positivity. When you feel positive emotions, it also shows in your body language. Experiencing them will increase your confidence and make others want to be around you.

The National Library of Medicine published an article exploring positive emotions' role in psychology. Essentially, positive emotions are contagious. When you feel good, others feel good too. Be happy, smiling, and laughing to make others smile and laugh too. Encourage people with positive words like "good job" or "nice hair" to help them feel good about themselves and build trust. By contrast, when you are feeling down or upset, it is hard for people to counter that mood. So if you have a negative comment to make, it's best to keep it to yourself.

### 11. Be Open about Your Flaws

Revealing your flaws is one of the best ways to make people like you. When people have a difficult time connecting with someone - and then they see that person's flaws - they might naturally be more open to taking a chance because having flaws makes you a real and relatable person. Plus, they will be more likely to feel sorry for you and want to help you out in some way. This is especially true if they have similar struggles. In addition, it can also make them more likely to like and trust you. Revealing your flaws doesn't mean that everyone has to know everything about you, though. You can choose to only show certain things or share things with certain people. For example, if you know that someone at work is struggling with something, mention that you, too, struggle with the same thing. This will help create a sense of comradery. This technique is especially useful for those already in a leadership role. In psychology, it's called the Pratfall Effect. It has been found that highly competent people are more likable when they make a mistake.

### 12. Be Vulnerable

Being vulnerable makes you more likable because it shows that you are willing to put yourself out there. By opening up about your past, you also show that you have trust and empathy for other people. This makes people feel more connected to you and more likely to like you. To be vulnerable, you need to be honest. Mistruths will make others feel uncomfortable, so it is best to trust your gut. This can be hard at first, but it will become easier with practice. To influence others with this quality, be honest and in tune with your emotions. Show that you can be open and honest about your feelings, fears, and concerns. When you are vulnerable, you are more likely to be perceived as likable and trustworthy.

### 13. The Psychology of Touch

It's really as simple as it sounds. Touching people shows that you care about them, and it makes them feel more comfortable opening up to you. In fact, touching is one of the most effective ways to make people feel close to you and create a connection. This is because physical contact releases the happy chemicals serotonin, oxytocin, and dopamine in your brain. It can be as simple as a gentle pat on the shoulder or a brush against the back. *Subliminal touching* is known to cause feelings of calmness, relaxation, and well-being.

While there are some situations where touching is inappropriate, like when working in an office or professional setting, in general, it's a great way to build rapport with other people but remember, touch doesn't mean grabbing! It's okay to lightly hold hands, touch arms or shoulders, or place your hand on someone's back to show that you're open to talking with them and that you care about their well-being.

## 14. Use Mirroring

Mirroring in psychology refers to the conscious matching of another person's behavior, thoughts, and feelings of others to reflect what the other person is doing or feeling. It is a form of emotional contagion in which one person's emotional state can influence the other person. When we mirror another person, we take their cues and follow suit by expressing deep empathy and understanding for their thoughts and emotions. By mirroring others, we are letting them know they are safe to be themselves and showing them that we care about them. Doing this can create a sense of connection with that person, which is why it's often used in therapy. A positive interaction that is relational mirrored can lead to mutual understanding, closeness, trust, and new relationships.

By understanding how people think, you can use several techniques to persuade them to take actions they might otherwise be reluctant to take. Do this by gaining their trust to increase the perceived value of you or your idea and drive up support for it.

There are also many benefits to using psychological tricks beyond just building rapport with your audience. For example, they can help you develop empathy. By taking a closer look at other people's problems, you'll be better able to understand why they might be interested in you or your service. At the same time, you'll have an opportunity to put yourself in their shoes and see things from their perspective. This will make it easier for you to empathize with them and show them that you care about them.

# Chapter 7: The Art of Listening without Judgement

Mastering the skill of attentive listening will help you succeed in many spheres of life, from school and work to relationships and friendships. This chapter will discuss the value of good listening abilities, the challenges of developing such skills, strategies for doing so, and techniques for listening with complete attention. You will also learn how to practice non-judgmental listening.

Everyone, from your closest circle of friends and family to your employees and the people you pass on the street, will benefit from clear and effective communication. It's necessary to be consistent, but it's equally necessary to remember that people communicate differently.

Being an attentive listener is a skill that will help you gain people's trust.
*https://unsplash.com/photos/Sp1uQo368fA*

Listening without passing judgment is a skill that is part of the skill set mental health professionals and counselors learn in their studies. Although training in this area has recently expanded to include mental health first responders, it is becoming more crucial that we all know how to listen effectively without passing judgment.

Understanding how important it is to listen without passing judgment is essential in emergencies (like stopping someone from thinking about suicide) and in everyday interactions with people who are in emotional pain.

Having the art of non-judgmental listening could stop a person's mental health crisis from worsening and assist them in getting the help that could change their lives.

# Active Listening: What Does It Mean?

It takes work to become active listeners; it's not something that comes naturally. The only way to become proficient is to put in the time and effort to learn it and apply it regularly.

When we listen actively, we pay close attention to what the other person is saying and take it in without forming our own opinions.

# What Is Non-Judgmental Listening?

Non-judgmental listening is listening without making judgments and being able to separate our feelings from a topic while listening.

Everyone has a "framework of reference"—a set of mental anchors from which to make decisions. The phrase "our framework of reference," first used by Aaron and Jacqui Schiff, describes the unique perspective through which each of us perceives the world.

Education, personal experiences, and views are just a few components that make up your unique frame of reference.

Without realizing it, your frame of reference shapes how you look at the world, and it can be hard to stay objective and keep your thoughts and opinions in check when faced with something that goes against your core beliefs.

One of the key things we can do to understand how to listen with empathy without being judgmental is to learn how to break free from this frame of reference so we can focus freely and honestly on the person we are listening to.

## Obstacles to Effective and Non-Judgmental Listening

These days, it's hard to pay attention to what someone's saying without being distracted by something else—the TV, the radio, the sound of the car engine, the buzz of a computer screen, or other commonplace items.

Moreover, even when we try to listen, we often do it mindlessly, agreeing without understanding the meaning of the words.

When someone's point of view differs from yours, you might be ready to make a snap judgment. You could try to dominate the discussion by talking over the other person or plotting your response while they are still talking.

Due to your self-absorption, you tend to focus on your own needs and ideas and pay less attention to the speaker. This self-centered outlook could be a result of bias, previous experiences, hidden objectives, or internal dialogue.

Mistaken assumptions, giving advice or analysis that wasn't asked for, denial, and feelings of fear, indifference, envy, or defensiveness can make it hard to listen effectively and without judging.

## The Essential Elements of Non-Judgmental Listening

There are three things a listener must do to create a secure space where a speaker feels comfortable opening up. The speaker could have difficulties opening up and sharing what they have to say if they don't have these ingredients.

### Acceptance

The most challenging aspect of reducing your frame of reference is learning to accept changes. Even if the speaker's ideas and experiences are different from yours, you need to be able to accept, tolerate, and understand them.

### Empathy

To empathize, you must first listen carefully to the other person without interrupting your thoughts or feelings. The best way to empathize with someone is to put yourself in their shoes so that you see things from their point of view and have a more nuanced understanding of the issue.

### Genuineness

You should mirror the other person's body language to convey your sincerity to them. Claiming to comprehend while displaying closed, uncaring body language sends the wrong message and fails to demonstrate open, non-judgmental listening.

## What Are the General Advantages of a Non-Judgmental Mindset?

Non-judgmental mindfulness entails paying close attention to the present moment without trying to change it.

The sense of liberation and calm resulting from connecting with this experience is worth seeking. There are several advantages to this as well. They include the following:

### Being Judgment-Free Allows You to Appreciate Life's Splendor

When you label something as "normal," it suggests it isn't worth your time. However, when you remove that "normal" label, you open yourself up to the possibility of seeing the marvel and splendor in every facet of life.

If you give something your full attention, you might get so much from it that it will change the way you see the world.

### Non-judgmental Listening Can Help You Get off the Hedonistic Adaptation

The constant pursuit of more is a significant source of discontent. The belief that what you have is insufficient drives the pursuit of more—whether in material goods, social status, or some other kind of success.

If you can stop this endless pursuit, you'll be able to see the many benefits of your current situation.

### It Is a Great Way to Calm Your Thoughts

You only have yourself to blame for worrying about the "unfortunate" things that have happened to you or that might happen.

If you can remove the "unfortunate" label, you'll be free of the anguish that comes with seeing the world through that lens.

### It Allows You to View Things the Way They Are

You only perceive the world as it appears to you based on how you react to your preconceived notions. Putting these aside will allow you to view things for what they are.

## Why Is Non-Judgmental Listening Important?

Since we are built to see the world through the lens of our preconceived notions, developing the ability to listen without passing judgment on what we hear requires time and effort.

However, there are many advantages to developing the skill of non-judgmental listening while seeking to help and comprehend people. They are as follows:

- It establishes an atmosphere where individuals feel secure enough to freely share their thoughts and feelings
- It provides a secure space where the speaker can explore and gain insight into their emotions and ideas about the topic
- Listening without passing judgment and showing empathy improves a person's mental health, which is crucial since it can lead to them getting the help they need

## How Can You Train Yourself to Listen More Intently?

The following are some suggestions for improving your effective listening abilities:

### Pay Close Attention

Are you meeting and conversing with someone? Try to be there physically and mentally, and pay close attention to the person speaking.

If this is a video chat, dismiss or remove all other browsers and turn off notifications to ensure you can focus on the conversation. Close the door, silence your phone, and lean in closer to the other person.

### Pay Attention to Nonverbal Clues

Can you tell if the person speaking is happy? How do they present themselves? What is their tone of voice telling you? Pay attention to such subtleties because they can greatly improve the conversational experience.

Just as the speaker's actions put them at ease and develop a real connection, so can yours (like maintaining eye contact, making facial gestures, or nodding to indicate you agree).

### Avoid Interfering

Interruptions are unquestionably the number one enemy of attentive listening. They show that you are not paying attention to what the other person is saying and that you believe your opinions are more valuable. Furthermore, it prevents you from following the speaker's train of thought and fully understanding the topic being discussed.

Therefore, take it easy, listen attentively and with patience, and let the other person finish speaking before you do, even if you believe it's your turn to speak.

### Ask Questions

It's appropriate to show curiosity, get clarity, and keep the discussion going by asking questions. Furthermore, if the conversation veers off subject, asking the correct questions might help get it back on course.

Remember to avoid cutting in. Wait for a gap in the discourse before launching into your questions.

### Summarize

In addition to showing that you've been paying attention, quoting or summarizing significant points of the discussion helps you and the other person consider whether you've interpreted the topic accurately.

You can both emphasize what's important and provide specific next steps.

# How Can You Develop the Skill of Non-judgmental Listening?

It takes some time and effort to develop the skill of non-judgmental listening.

Here are some suggestions to help you start developing your ability to listen without passing judgment:

### Examine Your Mental Condition

It's crucial to ensure you're in the appropriate mood to actively listen to someone else so you can hear what they have to say.

Sometimes we have trouble listening to others because we are upset with ourselves or because something bad has happened recently. When you're listening to someone, keep your mind calm and open your heart so you can absorb any information.

### Make Sure You're Exhibiting the Appropriate Attitude

Acceptance, authenticity, and empathy are the three pillars of non-judgmental listening, and all three must be present for effective empathic listening.

When you have a receptive mindset, you acknowledge and cherish the speaker's perspective without questioning the reality of their emotions, experiences, or beliefs.

This mindset helps you put yourself in the subject's shoes, making you more authentic and empathic.

### Use Your Oral Listening Abilities

Subtly expressing interest in a conversation can help reduce the likelihood of either party feeling the need to interrupt.

Excellent verbal listening skills include:

- Ask crucial questions to confirm your knowledge
- Using cues like "yeah, sure" and "I see."
- Giving someone time to think before continuing
- Summarizing what they've said
- Echoing their sentiments

These gestures show that you are paying close attention to what the other person is saying.

### Employ Non-Verbal Listening Skills

You can also demonstrate that you can listen without interrupting or offering your opinion through your actions.

Understanding body language is essential for non-verbal communication. The ability to demonstrate attentiveness through body language is a highly effective tool. One example of this would be to avoid crossing your arms, which might give the impression that you are being unfriendly or closed off to what is being said.

One way to display a pleasant body language signal is to make eye contact with the other person at a respectful distance. You should also sit instead of stand, give each other enough personal space, and arrange your seats so that you are not exactly across from one another.

Small gestures, like nodding your head, will show the person that you are paying attention. Allowing for natural, comforting silences and supporting spaces can give the person a moment to reflect.

### Understand, but Do Not Dismiss, the Speaker

Suppose you interrupt the speaker too often, finish their sentences, make irrelevant comments, or take over the conversation with stories about your own life. In that case, it will detract from what they are saying and stop the speaker's willingness to open up.

If you go into a discussion without preconceived notions about what the other person will say or how you will respond, you'll foster a more open atmosphere. Be receptive and give the person time to talk.

Keep your opinions and experiences to yourself until the conversation has progressed to a level where you can share your experiences appropriately to show that you understand the speaker's position.

### Cultural Differences Must Be Respected

Culture plays a big role in interpreting verbal and nonverbal cues, such as appropriate body language and personal boundaries. If you want to ensure you're communicating clearly, you can ask the other person when and with whom they feel most at ease.

Understanding cultural distinctions might help you listen to someone of a different ethnicity or cultural background without passing judgment.

### Visualize the Speaker's Words in Your Mind

To better understand what you're hearing, give your mind some time to develop a picture in your head. If you keep your mind clear and your senses active, your brain will do the rest, whether you're trying to form an image in your head or arrange your thoughts.

Focus on and memorize important terms and phrases while you're listening to someone. It's disrespectful to prepare your response mentally while someone else is talking, so put your thoughts to the back of your mind when it's time to listen.

Finally, recall what is stated, even if it appears boring or insignificant. When your mind starts to wander, remind yourself to bring it back.

### Please Provide Feedback

Show that you comprehend the speaker's perspective by mirroring their feelings. All you have to do is nod your head and make sounds of agreement to show that you agree with what is being said.

The speaker needs to see that you are paying attention to what they are saying. In cases where the speaker's feelings are hidden or their words are ambiguous, asking them to repeat themselves could be necessary to ensure you get the whole meaning.

### Keep an Open Mind

If you judge someone while they're speaking, you will not be able to help them at all. Simply listen without forming an opinion.

If what they say makes you uneasy, don't let it influence your reactions. Remember you are trying to be an effective and helpful listener, not a judge and jury in which you come up with a retort or draw comparisons to other people.

Listen without making assumptions. Remember that the person making these remarks will likely reveal their innermost thoughts and emotions to you.

You can only learn about such feelings and ideas by listening since you have no concept of what they are.

# Improving Listening Skills through Mindfulness

Mindful listening helps us become more sensitive to the speaker's intentions while maintaining an open mind. The practice of mindfulness will help you become a better listener.

### What Is Mindful Listening?

Mindfulness is paying attention in a certain way: consciously, in the present moment, and without judgment. It is especially effective in enhancing romantic relationships since we are more inclined to respond instinctively and emotionally.

Through practicing mindfulness, one can tune into your immediate surroundings, let go of unnecessary thoughts and feelings, and regulate their reactions to the words of others in a better manner. A lack of awareness can make you susceptible to your own biases and prevent you from paying attention to what the speaker is saying by acting as a distraction from your focus on those things.

After a few moments, the average person remembers only twenty-five percent of what is said in a speech. The goal of practicing attentive listening is to stop thinking about yourself, so you can fully understand what the other person is saying.

## How to Listen Mindfully

The following suggestions can assist you in incorporating mindfulness into your everyday interactions and improving your connections with others:

### Listen Carefully

We routinely participate in activities and connect with people without much consideration.

Practicing mindfulness means paying undivided attention to the speaker. There are numerous approaches to this:

- **Give yourself some breathing space:** If you need a moment to collect your thoughts before a meeting, take one. Mentally scan your body and relax your muscles before you approach the person.

- **Meditate:** Meditation is a mindfulness practice that helps you train your mind to pay more attention to the present moment. Mindfulness training can guide you to declutter your thoughts and make way for new ideas and insights.

  You'll find that meditation, like other forms of physical activity, becomes easier the more you practice it. Meditation can be hard to fit into a busy schedule, but even a few minutes a day can help.

- **Simplify your environment:** Many people get sidetracked at work because of their phones, laptops, or printers. Keep your workstation clear and switch off all electronic gadgets.

## Take Note of Your Cues

Our emotional and physiological responses, such as worry or irritation, can serve as cues and cause us to ignore or reject ideas and perspectives we find unappealing. If you are aware of your signals and choose to ignore them, you'll be able to communicate with others much better.

However, when you train your mind to be present and aware, you can listen without being affected. For instance, you might feel a tightening in your chest if the speaker says something you strongly disagree with. You might respond to this distressing experience without practicing mindfulness and end up saying something you regret.

## Listen with Empathy

We often filter reality through the lens of our biases and experiences. One of the benefits of developing empathy is the possibility of gaining insight into a situation from another person's viewpoint.

You could, for example, legitimize the other person's opinion by recognizing it. You don't have to accept their perspective to acknowledge it as valid; you just need to realize that it's different from your own.

The strategies described above are equally useful in one's personal life and career. A few of these tips might be more applicable at different times, but overall, using them will make you a more focused and approachable person.

This is why it's crucial to have an open mind while considering other people's communication methods. It's important to remember that the individuals you interact with in your professional and personal life come from many walks of life and have had varying life experiences.

The skills and knowledge you acquire in school and on the job are crucial, as are interpersonal skills such as respect, listening, and teamwork.

# Chapter 8: Asking the Right Questions at the Right Time

While listening without judging is the right approach to building trust, it's merely the first step in personality development. To let your charisma shine, you must learn the art of asking the right questions at the right time. Without a doubt, asking questions improves learning and facilitates the exchange of ideas. A novel study led by psychological scientists reveals asking questions puts a positive impression and boosts communication skills.

Learn to ask the right questions to open people up to you.
https://www.pexels.com/photo/two-women-holding-pen-601170/

For some individuals, asking the right questions comes naturally due to attributes like heightened emotional intelligence, inquisitiveness, and the ability to read people. In contrast, most of us need clarification about where to begin. Here's what you need to know to ask the right questions and build on your captivating persona.

# The Art of Asking the Right Question

Only some people know what and how to ask. While it may simple enough, asking good questions takes effort and time to perfect. You might wonder if asking the right question will get you the correct answer the moment you ask. It might be confirmed when the information you are seeking is specific.

However, you may need to follow up with relevant questions in other situations. A good question will direct the conversation straight to the point, as it's descriptive and concise and shows the person truly understands what you mean. Before we get into the details, let's quickly review the three questions you will use.

### Open-ended Questions

These questions trigger the listener's thoughts and motivate them to think and respond appropriately. This way, the listener expresses more of their thoughts or shares their opinion related to the question.

### Follow-Up Questions

This type of question is of fundamental importance when carrying out a conversation. Typically, follow-up questions follow a format where the questions are asked about the topic or issue, moving towards more specific questions at the end.

### Leading Questions

Leading questions are more likely to steer the conversation in the direction you want. Using them will let you get the type of response you want. However, you won't get accurate information or expression of what the listener wants to say. For example, you want to ask a friend for their review about a restaurant's buffet you attended a week ago. Posing the question, ' Hey, what do you think about the terrific food we had at the buffet last week' will get you a biased answer and limit the listener from giving you their opinions.

Depending on the purpose of the conversation and the context, these three categories can be used accordingly to achieve effective results.

# Why Is Asking the Right Questions at the Right Time Necessary?

Most people stick to their assumptions, inhibiting themselves from learning as they are invested in their beliefs and don't welcome another perspective or opinion on a particular matter. This behavior restricts their ability to learn and engage and shows a complete lack of curiosity. Likewise, some individuals feel unsure or uncertain about the questions, fearing the questions they ask could portray them as ignorant or having poor knowledge. Look around, and you'll find that all the great leaders are always asking questions and always open to learning. Approaching with the right questions at the right place assists you in several ways mentioned below.

- Whether you are negotiating with a friend, family member, neighbor, or co-worker, no matter the person or their relationship, asking questions eventually builds up a connection of trust and understanding. It allows you to connect in a meaningful manner.
- Questions are asked to seek meaningful insights. This approach helps develop a deeper understanding of the matter and any issues that need to be addressed.
- When you ask the right questions, the other person will automatically be engaged in the conversation, seeing it as relevant. They will perceive you as a competent and understanding person and be more open to you.
- In a workplace setting, asking the right questions at the right time provokes a sense of responsibility where the worker will consider their contribution and solve the issue quickly.
- It provides valuable insights, and you can maintain a problem-solving approach to achieve fruitful outcomes, benefiting you and the other person involved in the conversation.
- Asking questions at the right time reduces the chances of making mistakes, boosts your negotiating skills, and allows you to identify any potential situations that might need to be addressed.

Timing your questions is imperative. If you start a discussion in an inappropriate environment, the listener won't be comfortable listening to you, might not pay attention, and even ignore what you are asking. Therefore, depending on the situation, ask yourself whether it's the right time to pose a question or if you should wait and approach them at another better time.

Effective questioning is powerful and thought-provoking since the questions are open-ended. Adding different types of questions might make other people defensive and unwilling to answer. So questions should be thought-provoking and helpful to generate the right approach. For example, if a workplace has to solve an issue and you are in a bad position, ask them what could be the possible solution rather than assuming employees know about the subject.

Solving problems, learning, building relationships, influencing others, and research can all be done with effective questioning.

# How Will Asking Appropriate Questions Get People to Like Me?

In social gatherings or public meetups, if people can't think of something engaging to talk about, they'll focus on the other person and start asking questions which can sometimes become too awkward. A paper published by the *Journal of Personality and Social Psychology* reveals that most people are inclined to resolve their issues rather than be receptive and willing to listen. However, if you flip the focus to the person in front of you and approach with relevant questions, it will positively impact the other person, and they will see you as competent and reliable. Here's a step-by-step process to carry out a meaningful conversation and get people to admire your personality.

### Getting Started

Asking the right question involves two significant factors: timing and the question's relevancy. What you ask needs to be subtle rather than just another way of starting a conversation. While numerous studies advocate the effectiveness of asking open questions for a better conversation, it's imperative to ask a relevant question to steer the relationship on the right track.

The timing of the question is also crucial. Suppose the other person is already lost in their own thoughts or issues. In that case, it's more likely the conversation will end without any fruitful results. Therefore, ensure you pick the right time to ask a question.

Furthermore, if you feel the other person wants to ask a question, be open, listen to them first, and be helpful as you can. This will free their mind from thoughts clouding their thinking ability. Not listening to them and asking questions will take you nowhere.

To leave a positive impact, focus on asking rather than instructing, telling, or posing a direct question. They might listen, accept, or completely ignore the conversation if you tell someone. However, their brain will compel them to respond when you ask them about their take on the question. This shows a question's influence as opposed to directly telling people what they ought to do. Let's review different approaches you can practice to better ask questions with meaningful outcomes.

### Figuring Out What You Want to Know

Before asking anything, choose the correct wording, aiming for opinions, advice, or facts. Start by thinking about what you want to know. Being relevant and subtle is crucial as it will steer towards a more specific answer. That way, you'll catch the other person's interest and put them in a comfortable position where they will be open to the discussion. Asking questions they might not be willing to answer can take the conversation instantly downhill.

### Choosing the Right Person to Ask

Depending on what you are aiming to ask, choose the person accordingly. Don't barge in with questions. Instead, ask politely whether they are available to answer some questions. If they agree, it's the best time to ask as they'll be more open to listening and understanding what you have to say. Furthermore, talking with the right person results in fruitful results in terms of better engagement.

### Waiting for an Answer

Stay composed when a conversation is in progress, and avoid speeding it up after you've asked questions. Give the person adequate time to respond. Even if you want to carry out a healthy conversation, barging in with follow-up questions without listening to the answers will make them think you don't value their perspective. After they have finished answering, you can carry out a further conversation with follow-up questions to gain clarification on the matter. Using active listening skills is beneficial and leaves a positive impression.

### Following Up with Questions

It's best to carry on with the conversation and ask follow-up questions. Unless you are seeking facts, the question you will ask might be influenced by assumptions. Therefore, continuing with a follow-up question helps learn more about the situation and instills a positive image. However, staying highly relevant and specific is crucial while asking in a friendly tone. A review study published in the Journal of Personality and Social Psychology found that asking appropriate follow-up questions improves the interpersonal bond with the person asking the question. Choosing the wrong questions will make the other person defensive, whereas keeping the conversation friendly and asking the right questions highlights your desire to be informed about the situation.

Ensure the questions you ask to show your curiosity and willingness to know more about the issue. These follow-up questions can be probing questions that automatically get the other person involved more profoundly in the discussion. Questions like these spark curiosity, promote critical thinking and allow you to receive genuine feedback from people on how they feel about a particular matter.

### Thanking the Person

Finish the conversation by thanking them for their response and time. Ensure your body language and the way of engagement highlights your appreciation for them. Showing gratitude and thankfulness further strengthens a relationship and allows you to seek help, assistance, or guidance whenever required. While the process will work for almost every scenario, you may want to tweak it depending on the situation's circumstances and severity. For example, engaging in a casual conversation with your co-worker differs from asking niche-specific questions in a corporate meeting.

## Tips for Asking the Right Questions

### Avoiding Rhetorical Questions

Asking irrelevant or rhetorical questions just for the sake of making conversation or emphasizing a specific matter should be avoided at all costs. Make a quick strategy or think of relevant questions you can ask to receive the necessary information you want while keeping it on the right track.

### Be Open and Understanding

Be mindful of what you ask the other person, and work on understanding their mindset and ability to answer. Posing questions that put the person in an awkward position is not a good idea. Furthermore, ensure you ask the questions in the right setting. Doing this will help you get the response you hope to get from the conversation.

### Practicing Active Listening

Implement what you've learned in the previous chapters, like maintaining a positive attitude, smiling, nodding, and showing engagement through eye contact. To clear any misunderstanding, engage with probing questions and politely paraphrase their answer after they have completed confirming whatever you've listened to.

### Pausing and Using Silence

It's crucial to be patient and use silence instead of asking unnecessary questions. Pauses between questions allow the other person to relax and be comfortable while engaging with you. You should start by getting yourself and the other person in your comfort zone, asking a question, and then waiting for them to respond. Listen to them with utmost attention when they speak, and wait some more before asking follow-up questions. Many times, if you give an individual enough time, the chances are the person will likely give you more information.

### Avoiding Interruptions

Never interrupt a person talking with you. It gives a negative impression that you don't value their opinion and reject what they have to say. Stopping them while they are talking might steer the conversation the way you want, but it will never go as intended. However, when time is limited, you may interrupt only when the other person is straying from the topic. Still, be polite and show respect while redirecting the conversation with a relevant question.

### Asking How You Would Want to Be Asked

Think about how you would like others to approach you and act the same as you would expect things to be. Keeping this mindset allows you to sieve through questions and avoid asking what might result in an issue.

### Having a Clear Mind

Assuming can influence a person's thoughts based on these assumptions, leading to a different conclusion and not the one they intended. Keep away from assumptions, and be unbiased to achieve the maximum impact.

### Avoid Asking Binary Questions

Make sure you don't put forward a question whose answer is a simple yes or no. You can use this approach when closing a conversation, but it should always be avoided, especially when the discussion has already started. Starting with a binary question will lead you to need more information. Avoid using the phrases would, should, is, and are in questions. Instead, switch to who, where, when, and how to influence people to think and provide relevant information.

### Speaking the Language

Brainstorm when preparing questions and ensure you are asking queries that the person can easily understand. Ask while considering their frame of reference and pick familiar words or phrases for easy understanding. For example, using industry-specific terminology with someone outside your industry will get you nowhere. Furthermore, focus on using neutral wording.

### Sticking to the Essentials

If you already understand and know what you expect the answer to be, consider avoiding asking it. This will save time. Remember to build a series of questions, from asking general questions and moving to specific questions moving forward.

### Asking One Question at a Time

While in a conversation, ensure you ask one question at a time rather than putting multiple queries on the table. Keeping to this strategy will mean that communication is clear and understandable. It will present you as a person who approaches the issues logically and has a deep understanding. Here's how you can stick to asking one question at a time.

- If it's an important event like a meeting, write down the questions you'll be asking so you remember
- Being patient, listening to the person, and adding a follow-up question when relevant

Gaining expertise in asking the right questions takes time, the right approach, and lots of practice. It's never guaranteed that your questions will get you closer or farther from your objectives. The simplest way to be good at asking questions is by starting to ask. Time and practice will sharpen your skill. Remember that fruitful outcomes will only be possible when you ask good questions.

# Chapter 9: Twelve Ways to Be More Interesting

It comes as no surprise that fascinating individuals are generally popular and well-liked. Being an interesting person is an inborn trait - it comes easily and effortlessly to those who inherit it. For others, however, being intriguing is not as easy. Luckily, there are several things that you can do to project the image of being more interesting and appealing.

In this chapter, you'll learn why it's a positive thing to be interesting and how this trait puts you at an advantage. You'll also come across a list of things you can do to develop this characteristic.

## Advantages of Being Interesting

Before we go into how you can be a more intriguing person, let's explore some of the advantages of being such a person. Engaging people are generally fun to spend time with. When you're interested, people will want to spend time with you. There's never a dull or awkward moment around fascinating people.

Compelling individuals naturally attract the attention of others. They easily stand out and appear different from others. Being more interesting can also help you land jobs more easily. Interesting people are usually adventurous, experienced, and authentic. They enjoy sharing their discoveries with others, never stop learning, and don't like to do things just because everyone else is doing them. Besides field knowledge, qualifications, and expertise, these characteristics are among every employer's ideal candidate list. Not only are interesting people fun and easy to work with, they always have new and fresh ideas. They are assets to the organizations and contribute to enriching their organizations' cultures.

Interesting people never miss opportunities and experiences and don't shy away from challenges. The fear of failure or rejection seldom holds them back. The way they present themselves confidently at every opportunity contributes to their success and helps them get better positions at work. This risk-taker quality they possess helps them make more money, as well. Appealing people don't need to lie to impress others. They've also usually seen more of life than others, allowing them to understand the things that truly matter. This is why they're generally very humble, friendly, and down-to-earth and know better than to let their egos soar, which makes them more trustworthy and honest, and helps them build healthy and fulfilling relationships along the way.

Fascinating people are hard to forget. They always leave unique and intriguing impressions on others which leads to them having a large professional and social network and gives them an edge at job interviews. Most importantly, being an interesting person can make you happier and healthier. It's hard not to thrive mentally, emotionally, and physically when you have the key to elevating your life's personal, social, and professional aspects.

## How to Be More Interesting

### 1. Learn a New Skill

Learning a new skill is one way to make yourself appear more appealing to others. You don't need to learn how to fly a helicopter to sound interesting (although you should definitely give it a try if that's what you want to do). This new skill can be as simple as learning a new language or taking up a new sport. You can also take an introductory course in a topic you're interested in, such as psychology, trading NFTs, fashion design, or digital marketing, and continue learning about it if you find it right for you.

The skill you choose to develop doesn't have to be related to your current studies or industry. Make a list of things you've always wanted to try, even as a child, and start from there. Set your goal and devise a plan to help you get there. If you decide to take up a sport, search for recommendations for instructors in your area. Watch training sessions and ask the instructor what to expect as a beginner, the average learning curve, and so on.

If you're taking a language or other educational course, decide whether you'll be enrolling in a physical or online classroom. Weigh out each alternative's pros and cons before making a decision.

When you start learning, you may feel compelled to absorb more information or go at a faster pace than you're supposed to. However, effective learning can be achieved by taking small and steady steps forward. Remember the 80/20 rule: 80% of the outcomes result from 20% of the inputs. In other words, don't underestimate the effort that you invest, no matter how little it seems.

To develop a new skill, you must learn a set of sub-skills in the process. Let's say you decide to take up horse riding as a sport. While you'll be learning how to ride horses and maybe even jump obstacles, you'll notice that your body coordination, critical and quick thinking, memory, and decision-making skills are improving over time. Horse riding is also associated with self-confidence, compassion, and excellent non-verbal communication skills. If you take art classes, your hand-eye coordination, creativity, imagination, and motor skills will improve.

## 2. Stay Curiosity and Don't Stop Asking Questions

There's nothing interesting about passive people who take the world around them for granted. You merely exist when you don't observe the environment around you, ask questions, and actively seek answers. Instead of interacting with the universe, you accept whatever it throws your way. This is a surefire way to silence your voice and blend in with everyone around you.

Curiosity is the essence of creativity. We don't get new ideas out of the blue, even if it sometimes seems like it. We can't be inspired by something we haven't seen or recognized before. If you aren't curious, plenty of ideas will probably fly right over your head because you've never trained your mind to pick up on them.

Curiosity exposes you to a new realm of opportunities you wouldn't notice otherwise. It also creates a diversion in a routine-driven life. Curious people find adventures in the most unexpected places.

To nurture your curiosity, you need to be open to learning new things and change how you think about certain things. Curious people aren't scared to discover that some of their beliefs and knowledge may be wrong. They constantly try to dig deeper into the world's inner workings and understand why things are the way they are. They don't hesitate to ask as many questions as they need to get the information they're searching for. These questions may lead you toward new experiences and serve as engaging conversation openers. Being a curious person encourages you to acquire a great deal of general knowledge, which can be quite impressive.

### 3. Be a Great Storyteller

While awesome experiences, opportunities, and curious discoveries are crucial if you wish to be interesting, you will fail to capture other people's attention and leave the desired impression if you lack storytelling skills. The way you tell your stories needs to be engaging and captivating.

Good storytellers are organized and straight to the point. Imagine someone is telling you all about their trip to the moon- quite interesting, right? However, for some reason, they ramble on about how they were so conflicted about what to pack into their bag. They go into excruciating details regarding their ride to the space station. Just as they were finally about to tell you what the inside of the shuttle was like, they said, "oh! No, sorry, this isn't what happened. I had to run an errand before I went to the station...." They spend so much time going into useless details that you lose interest in a potentially riveting story.

Skilled storytellers know which details to stress and which ones to leave out. They know how to make a story sound more captivating than it actually is without having to make up any details. They are descriptive, can elicit emotions, and know how to speak in various tones and speeds to capture and maintain the listener's attention.

### 4. Share Your Passions with Others

Many people avoid talking about things they're passionate about, especially if they're not mainstream. Perhaps they've been told that no one cares or that they talk too much. However, passionate individuals draw the attention of others. It doesn't matter what you like - being enthusiastic about a certain topic and feeling excited to share your knowledge and experiences surrounding it causes people to find you interesting.

As counter-intuitive as it sounds, you get extra points for being passionate about something that isn't all that common or popular. While mainstream or common interests can spark deep conversations and great bonds with others, unconventional interests make people curious. They'll want to hear about the topic and understand why you're so passionate about it. Passions, hobbies, and talents make you memorable.

### 5. Be Honest and Outspoken

Interesting people don't like hopping on the bandwagon. They never adopt beliefs or ideas that don't align with their perceptions and values. They don't mind sharing their thoughts and ideas even when they're different than those around them. Be outspoken if you feel the need to be. This doesn't mean you should argue with anyone who has an opposing view, but it simply means that you should never be afraid of being authentic about your opinions. Even those who don't agree with you will respect your frankness.

### 6. Don't Mind the Opinions of Others

You should never worry about what other people think of you. While everyone feels compelled to hide certain parts of themselves or pretend to like or dislike things to gain the approval of others at times, no one should ever give in to this urge. Our unique differences are what make us interesting. Most importantly, it is the way that a person embraces their true self and refuses to mask any aspect of their being that makes them the most fascinating.

Don't hold yourself back or fear expressing your opinions and convictions just because you're worried that someone may not like them. People will always find something to criticize and dislike - you'll never be perfect for everyone. The most interesting individuals are those who maintain their authenticity regardless of who they're with, where they're at, or what they're doing.

### 7. Never Stop Learning

Knowledge is infinite - no amount can ever be enough. People who realize the countless possibilities in the universe and allow their curiosity to take the lead are the most exciting to be around. As someone who enjoys asking limitless questions, you give rise to thought-provoking conversations that keep everyone engaged. Being in a never-ending state of wonder can make you more knowledgeable, giving people the impression that you're highly intelligent and well-versed in various subjects.

Educational systems have conditioned us to think of learning as a burdensome process. If you continue to hold on to this belief, you will never feel compelled to dig deeper into any topic, even if you're interested in it. If you associate learning with something fun and advantageous, you'll naturally find yourself trying to learn more about a wide array of topics. It's not easy to shift your overall perception of learning overnight. It helps to think of learning as a neutral process that allows us to gain helpful knowledge before we can think of it as a fun and fulfilling experience.

### 8. Share What You Learn

Interesting individuals come across as having this trait because they enjoy sharing what they learn with others. They don't talk about their experiences because they're self-absorbed but because they want others to enjoy and learn from their discoveries. They like to talk about why a certain topic piqued their interest in the first place and what they learned about it along the way.

### 9. Be a Good Listener

People who lack good listening skills often come across as self-absorbed and uninterested in those around them. Individuals who only care about themselves and don't listen to what others say are *far from captivating*. While you should be a good conversationalist and aim to share your knowledge with others, you also need to find the right balance between speaking and listening

Few people realize that listening is a vital component of communication skills. You can't build an effective argument or get your point across if you don't fully understand the other person's point of view. When listening to a person, take the time to absorb and process their words. Reflect on what they're saying and reiterate in your own words. This shows others that you're invested in what they're saying and that you are having a two-way conversation. Being an active listener will help others determine if your storytelling efforts are genuine or if they're an excuse to show off your accomplishments.

## 10. Prioritize Self-Development

Nothing is more attractive than a person who prioritizes growth and development. Set a goal for yourself that you wish to achieve and devise a strategy that can help you work toward it. Practicing visualization techniques can help you let go of unhelpful thought patterns. Imagining your life after accomplishing everything you want to achieve can help you stay motivated and driven.

When working towards self-development, you should try to keep positive. Keep track of all your thoughts and notice when intrusive ones start making their way into your headspace. Meditate, imagine the negative thoughts vaporizing into thin air, or try any other distraction. The most important thing is that you cut these thoughts off before they grow more powerful.

Practicing meditation and mindfulness techniques for as little as five minutes a day can prove to be very effective when dealing with negative situations. These exercises can teach you to regulate your breathing and take control of your mind and the thoughts that wander through it.

You'll likely experience numerous setbacks on your journey to self-growth. Remind yourself that you shouldn't let these inconveniences discourage you from moving forward. Think of them as more opportunities for learning and growth instead. Celebrate and reward yourself each time you overcome a small challenge.

## 11. Be Your Only Competition

The least appealing people are those who view everyone else as a threat. Constantly competing with others prevents you from celebrating their successes, even if they're your closest friends. This slowly leads to feelings of resentment and can cause you to lose many people in your social circle. Toxic competition can be detrimental to your physical, emotional, and mental health. This is why your only competition should be yourself.

We all have different opportunities and learning curves. Additionally, each one of us faces a unique set of obstacles and challenges along the way. Competing with others is impossible since you all live under different circumstances and operate in different environments. Focus on your own goal and weigh your progress against your previous performance. You're the only person who can tell whether you're on the right track.

There will come times when you'll find yourself lagging. Don't give up; aim for a consistent pace and remind yourself of the bigger picture and why you started working toward your goal in the first place. The more you reinforce this way of thinking, the easier you'll be able to incorporate this attitude into your personality. Don't forget to celebrate the small victories along the way.

There is nothing that people find more inspiring and interesting than a person driven toward a single goal who doesn't bother to compete with anyone other than themselves. This behavior is an indicator of self-confidence and awareness.

### 12. Leave Toxic Attitudes at the Door

If you want people to enjoy your company, you must know which attitudes to let go of. Overly negative individuals are energy vampires. No one likes to be around a person who constantly anticipates the worst and only talks about the negative aspects of their life.

Individuals who wait for success to be served to them on a silver platter are also very uninspiring. Passive individuals who don't actively move toward their goals will always fall behind and likely complain about it.

You should always avoid negative and self-deprecating talk. Don't tell yourself that you'll never be able to achieve your goals or succeed. Our subconscious minds absorb the thoughts and words that we feed ourselves, which is why they often become a reality. Reciting daily affirmations can help you reframe your thought process and become more optimistic.

Alluring people own up to their mistakes and take full responsibility for their behaviors and actions. They realize that faults don't diminish their self-worth, which is why they always confidently carry themselves. Avoid blaming others for any bad situations that you find yourself in.

Confident people also realize that asking for help is not a weakness, so they don't mind asking others for assistance. They understand that being too prideful can hinder their chances of success.

# What Makes an Interesting Person?

Now that you've learned about the advantages of being interesting and come across tips on becoming a fascinating individual, let's explore some of the traits that make an interesting person vs. an uninteresting one.

### An Interesting Person Is:

- Confident
- Assertive
- Has a strong sense of self
- Has high self-awareness
- Independent
- Passionate
- Creative
- A risk-taker
- Never stops learning
- Prioritizes self-growth and development
- Authentic
- Expressive
- Doesn't lose sight of their purpose
- Has goals
- Has a life purpose

### An Uninteresting Person Is:

- Self-centered
- Arrogant or egotistic
- Close-minded
- Not open to new experiences
- Fixated on certain ideologies and convictions
- Not willing to accept that they may be wrong
- A poor communicator
- Likely to take themselves too seriously

- Inflexible
- Not adaptable
- Highly predictable
- Uninterested in those around them

Being an interesting individual can help you build strong relationships and professional networks. It can give you a great advantage and help you get ahead. While some people are naturally interesting, you can acquire this trait by being authentic, goal-oriented, passionate, outspoken, and curious.

# Chapter 10: Dos and Don'ts When It Comes to Being Liked

Some people appear to be born with likable characters. These people find it easy to blend in with strangers, and opportunities seem to come their way easily. It's possible they picked up those characteristics as children without realizing it. The good news is that you can cultivate these characteristics to make yourself more appealing.

With family and friends, you can be yourself and flaunt all your flaws without worrying, and they will still love you, but with strangers, you will need to refine your personality. Throughout your life, you will meet and interact with thousands of people. Some are at school, while others are at work or social gatherings.

Being liked by others, especially those with whom you have a close relationship, can open doors to new opportunities. Your friends would be delighted to inform you of anything because it makes them feel comfortable and valued. Your coworkers will be glad to collaborate with you because it is the better option, and your boss may even promote you to reflect your abilities better. All of this is possible if you are liked.

To build strong relationships with others, you must have social intelligence. The characteristics that make you likable, as will be discussed in this chapter, will assist you in developing strong connections with people from various walks of life. Almost everything involving interacting with others requires a pinch of social intelligence.

Most of the time, the things you do wrong knowingly or unknowingly cause people to dislike you. Your friends and family are the only people who will accept you as you are because they have known you long enough to understand what you stand for. However, this is a small group of people when compared to the rest of your relationships.

In this chapter, you will learn about the mistakes you may have made that have harmed your relationships with others. Being liked cannot be overstated; while not everyone will like you, having a likable personality makes it easy for anyone to like you. As a result, you should deliberately cultivate characteristics that will make people like you. This chapter contains a comprehensive guide to achieving your ideal personality.

## The Do's to Make People Like You

People want to believe they can trust you with sensitive information and tasks. These tips will help you earn people's love and likeness, but you shouldn't expect too much in return because not everyone will like you - that's just life. Here are a few tips to follow:

### It Is Okay to Acknowledge Your Weaknesses

Whether you want to admit it or not, people will see through you and figure you out. No one wants to be associated with a liar, and denying your flaws will make you appear as someone who is hiding something and, therefore, not to be trusted. Sharing or acknowledging your vulnerability does not mean shouting your issues from the rooftops or that you should act helpless to win people's sympathy. It means that you must be aware of when the time is right to disclose information and be honest in all your dealings. Otherwise, you could end up ruining things even more.

You can admit a mistake you made due to ignorance when you are with friends. For instance, "Please accept my apologies, I was in a hurry and thought your slippers would fit me, but I ended up ruining them." This friend may have already known what you did and was waiting for you to come clean about it, but if you had denied your wrongdoings, that would have made you out to be a lying coward, and as a result, people will avoid you in the future.

When working with a team, you can show vulnerability by sharing what you find challenging and asking for help so everyone can win. This strategy makes everyone listening feel more at ease with their own flaws. Their perception of you will become positive and probably admiring because you dared to admit to your flaws. They will start to trust you with more opportunities and information. When you admit your shortcomings, others may offer you help, comfort, and assistance. Decide to embrace and talk about your flaws instead of keeping them hidden from anyone who cares to look; after all, we never stop improving.

### Avoid Being Pushy

People already have a lot on their shoulders, and you shouldn't add to it. Not being pushy is a difficult trait to master, but it is doable. Being flexible also entails not being intrusive. You will encounter people or situations who oppose what you can tolerate but try to compromise in such cases. Making tough choices often results in only some people liking your preferences.

For example, you may make a new friend who enjoys dancing and going to fun parks, but you would rather enjoy the peace of your surroundings than go to a noisy, fun place. At this point, sticking to your preferences will not make your new friend like you, but you can earn more of their favor by adjusting slightly to accommodate their preferences.

It doesn't mean you should give up what makes you happy! Rather, strike a balance between what you want and adjusting other people's preferences. You can tell new friends how you feel about loud places and tell them you are willing to give it a shot because of them. Being pushy and uptight will chase people from you because they either have to accept you or leave you.

### Lighten Up Your Mood

It is difficult to improve your mood if you're going through difficult times. You might have a lot going on in your life and need to think about it. Whatever good reasons you may have for being introverted and caught up with your feelings, it will be selfish of you to impose them on others. It would be tedious if you were with coworkers and all you think about and discuss are your problems!

Everyone has issues, but being able to put those problems aside and focus on the present will make people like you. Likable people are selfless with their emotions; they know when to set feelings aside. Pleasant people are always cheerful, and their smiles brighten the atmosphere. After completing your duties, seek solace among your friends, who will understand your emotions and be eager to assist you in finding a solution.

### Laugh as Often as Possible

Have you ever wondered why some people enter a room and immediately say or do things that make everyone laugh? People crave happiness and are drawn to anyone who can make them laugh easily. Likable people have carefree attitudes toward life.

You may not be the joking type, which is fine, but you can become more open to humor. Be the person who recognizes a joke for what it is and laughs it off. Close or distant associates would prefer a carefree individual who can easily smile and laugh. Not every statement or joke is meant to offend you, and finding fault with what people say around you can cause them to avoid you. Put on a happy face and make it easy for people to approach you.

### You Can't Know Everything – and the Sooner You Admit It, the Better

You wouldn't want to taste what the know-it-alls get. These people can be found in workplaces, schools, families, among friends, and anywhere else. If you are a know-it-all, people will most likely avoid you. People assume they know everything, possibly because no one offered to help them in their formative years, forcing them to learn everything they need to survive. But the social fallout is painful, so if you have this inclination, work on yourself to become more accommodating.

This group mistakenly believes they have spent too much time and money equipping themselves and cannot be wrong. They want everyone to think that whatever they say is the best. This attitude is unattractive and will make people dislike you. The know-it-all trait is common among leaders in various positions who want to impose their opinion on everyone. Still, you can be more accommodating to gain people's favor.

### Sincerely Care for Others

Developing a caring side may be challenging, especially if you feel you need your efforts to be recognized. We live in a time when most people believe the world and everything in it owes them something. You sometimes have to put your interests and goals aside to help others solve their problems if you want to be liked. It takes a significant amount of work to care for others.

Making others happy will require you to give up valuable resources like time or money. To avoid feeling guilty about your good deed, only help and don't expect anything in return. People will like you more if they realize your assistance isn't motivated by self-interest.

Helping people and expecting something in return will either ruin your chances of being liked or cause the admiration to be faked. It is a common trend on social media where you will see a popular person giving out gifts but getting little or no help when they are in need. It makes you wonder what happened to all the online love that was so evident whenever there was a gift to be shared. People can fake their emotions to continue receiving from you, so to overcome this and gain more followers, you should care for others with no expectations.

### Be a Good Listener

It's tempting to commandeer the conversations when you have a lot of interesting things to say, which is all fine and dandy, but you should take a break to allow others to contribute. Allowing for inclusiveness will make people like you more.

Communication is a two-way street, with one person speaking and the other listening. Being distracted when someone is speaking to you is not going to win you any friendships or acquaintances. Even if you don't like talking much, you can be the listening ear who encourages others to pour out their hearts as long as they know you will listen and respond. People will like you more if you listen to their opinions and are less judgmental. When you are the one speaking, try to give others space to respond and share their thoughts.

### Sacrifice Your Time

There are several doors that humility and taking a back seat will open for you, but don't attach strings. It's natural to admire someone who goes out of their way to help others even when they don't have to. People who are manipulative and supposedly give without expecting anything in return soon show their true colors when they figure out a way to make you pay back all the favors you've received. People will like you more if you are genuine in your sacrifice of time. Spending more time with people promotes familiarity – and people like people with whom they are familiar.

### Be Outspoken

You will need to express yourself clearly in a social setting. Don't expect anyone to read your mind and figure out your intentions. Talk as much as you need to when communicating your feelings and points. As a business owner, you must always speak plain English so your customers can understand and make informed decisions. Talking a lot is a strong character to be used when necessary. Avoid being a chatty person who interrupts conversations. Never pass up an opportunity to speak out, no matter how insignificant you believe the impact will be. Your speech could be the solution someone has been looking for, earning you more favor.

### Ask Questions

People will like you more when you give them the freedom to tell you everything they know. By allowing the other person to help you, you give them a sense of importance and boost the odds of them liking you. People will warm up to you quicker if you allow them to share their knowledge.

### Mirror the Other Person

Mirroring has assisted many people in reducing tension between strangers. This strategy involves mimicking another person's facial expressions, gestures, and body language. Be attentive and pick up on these details within the first few minutes of your conversation, then act them out. Mimicking other people's behavior can hasten being liked.

### Compliment Others

Complimenting others will not cost you anything. "I love your hair; it looks nice" or "you have a beautiful smile" can go a long way toward making people like you. People you compliment will subconsciously begin to see those qualities in you even if you don't have them. As you say nice things about others, they will start to think nice things about you. Try to do it sparingly; the key is to keep it moderate and genuine.

### Emit Positivity

Everyone around you could become unhappy if you are constantly angry and unhappy. Bad moods spread like wildfire. On the other hand, positive energy will show, and people will enjoy your company. Give out positive vibes to make yourself likable. Always look on the bright side of life and for reasons to be satisfied. Worry never solved a problem.

### Be a Competent and Warm Person

People will like you more if you are friendly and noncompetitive in the workplace or at other social gatherings. Nobody enjoys drama, which is why people are drawn to warming and welcoming people. People will like and respect you more if you are friendly and have a high educational or economic status. It would help if you got to know people before demonstrating your expertise. This point is especially pertinent in business environments where competition is unavoidable. Boasting your qualifications first may scare some people away or make them feel intimidated, making it difficult for them to associate with you.

### Emphasize Common Value

Being liked will show when people can identify with what you stand for. People will gravitate toward those with similar values over those who do not. This trait is primarily used by people seeking favor or public acceptance; you will hear stories about how they lived in a neighborhood similar to yours and experienced life the same way you do to get you to know and like them. Although some people employ this tactic maliciously, you can use it to benefit from the similarities you share with others.

### Share a Secret

People will like you more if you are vulnerable with them. Sharing a secret with someone makes them feel like they're a part of your life. You can make someone feel special and like you by confiding in them. Using this approach will help you get to know someone quickly, but don't share sensitive information too soon, particularly if you don't trust the person not to pass it on.

### Be Trust Worthy

The importance of sharing secrets in friendship building has already been discussed, but as a listener, you will be liked more if you can keep secrets entrusted to you. To be trustworthy means to be loyal, dependable, and truthful. People will easily like you if you possess these qualities.

# The Don'ts You Should Avoid for People to Like You

It's possible that you unintentionally irritate those around you. The following don'ts should be avoided if you want to develop a good relationship:

### When You Act Like You Dislike Someone

It would help to keep your body language in check to avoid sending the wrong message. People can't like you if you act as if you already dislike them.

### Not Smiling

Only some people have that friendly, smiling face, but you won't get people to like you if your face makes you appear unapproachable. It would help if you made an effort to smile and make welcoming gestures.

### You Are Too Nervous

People admire self-assurance and bravery. People attribute negative attributes to your nervousness, making you unlikeable.

### Bragging Too Much

You may be good at what you do, but try not to overestimate yourself, especially in front of strangers.

### You Are Too Nice

Being overly nice may give the impression that you are faking it. As no one is nice all the time, saying no every now and then will give you more credibility.

### You Hide Your Emotions

People cannot like you if they do not see you and be vulnerable. Appearing all-powerful and self-sufficient will not make you likable.

### Saying Nothing about Yourself But Aiming to Know More about Another Person

You can't build a good relationship if you hide everything about yourself. In exchange for all the personal information the other person provides, you must share a small portion of yourself.

### Sharing Deep Personal Information Early in Your Relationship

Before you share too much information with someone, you should understand how much they can handle. Otherwise, you risk turning them off.

### You Want to Always Be in Control

Trying to control everything around you and not letting people take ownership of anything is not going to make you popular. Give people a chance to show you what they can do.

### You Get Upset Easily

Getting upset and irritated easily will make you unapproachable, and you'll find yourself being avoided.

### You Talk Down to People

Who wants to be around someone who sees nothing good in them? There is no one. Instead of criticizing those around you, speak positively and encourage them.

### You Are Quick to Blame

Being less judgmental can be achieved by understanding the motivation behind an action. Look for causes before assigning blame.

### You Are Too Honest

While being honest is a virtue, there are times when it's best to keep quiet to avoid endangering anyone.

It is critical that people like you, even if it's not everyone. To make solid social connections, you need a healthy dose of people's appreciation. When you are well-liked, opportunities will come your way.

Try to make a good first impression when meeting strangers for the first time. If people misunderstand you the first time they meet you, it will take a long time for them to change their opinion of you. Make sure you use appropriate body language to convey your message. It's the little things we do naturally that make us appealing. As previously stated, people will respect you if you are confident and competent, and this book explains how you can achieve this level of proficiency.

You being charismatic means confidently showing your personality. When you present yourself with grace and courage, people admire you. You will draw a lot of attention wherever you go, and people can't help but like you. Be less judgmental around others, remembering that everyone is flawed in some way. Know when to ask questions and avoid crossing lines. You will become more interesting and likable after following every guide in this book.

The exercise that follows will assist you in applying everything you have learned from this book. Choose the best responses to fill in the blanks.

Mention five ways the first impression will help you build good social connections.

1._____
2._____
3._____
4._____
5._____

Mention three body language cues you'll start using to show off your charisma.

1._____
2._____
3._____

List four psychological tricks you have learned to make people like you.

1._____
2._____
3._____
4_____

Write down your plans for enhancing your listening abilities.

_____

What aspects of your attitude toward people should you change to become more interesting?

1._____
2._____
3._____
4._____
5._____

6._____
7._____
8._____
9._____
10._____

Sometimes you need to understand why you like someone so much. Perhaps the person checked all the boxes regarding what is required to be likable, but you didn't consider it. Your motivation may stem from the comfort you feel in the presence of such people. Liking someone is a psychological trick that many people unknowingly use. It involves a lot of effort, but it is worth it. In this chapter, we've highlighted tips and tricks to help you build better relationships.

# Conclusion

Have you realized how important it is that you are liked? This book contains a detailed guide and explanation to help you achieve your goal. Certain behaviors must be developed or fine-tuned if you already have them.

Sometimes you only have a few minutes to make an impression on a stranger. Your first impression will have a big influence on the meeting's outcome. You can make the atmosphere positive even if the stranger doesn't welcome you. Being liked gives you the ability to influence others easily. People will be considerate and welcoming to you because they like you. You will receive favors from strangers if they find you interesting.

Be deliberate in learning and applying the tips outlined in this book. The guides are written in simple terms and are easy to understand. Study and master modify gestures that do not correspond with the message you wish to convey.

Getting people to like you is a serious business that should be treated as such. Make the most of your first impression by giving strangers reasons to want to see you again. Be the one to brighten up a gloomy room with a smile or interesting conversation when you walk in. You could start casual conversations with everyone in the room to rouse them from their gloomy mood before shifting gears to make them laugh or smile. Be an approachable, empathetic, and dependable person that others can rely on for advice.

People admire charismatic people. It is safe to say that being there for others is the easiest way to gain their favor. Contribute as much as possible and participate in the small tasks they perform. You must improve your self-confidence to pitch your value to anyone, regardless of their economic status.

Don't assume you know everything; ask questions if you're confused. Asking questions does not mean that you make people repeat themselves ad nauseam. Only ask for clarification when necessary, and pay attention when someone is speaking to you.

Another quality that can endear you to others is your ability to listen. They will believe you genuinely care because you are interested in everything they say. Use their emotions to your advantage. It may appear at first that you are simply serving others or that you care deeply, but don't let this discourage you. Be kind without expecting anything in return. Maintain complete honesty at all times.

# Here's another book by Andy Gardner that you might like

# Free Bonus from Andy Gardner

Hi!

My name is Andy Gardner, and first off, I want to THANK YOU for reading my book.

Now you have a chance to join my exclusive email list related to human psychology and self-development so you can get the ebook below for free as well as the potential to get more ebooks for free! Simply click the link below to join.

P.S. Remember that it's 100% free to join the list.

Access your free bonuses here:
**https://livetolearn.lpages.co/how-to-make-people-like-you-paperback/**

# References

Kim, L. (2016, November 21). 14 things that will make people like you (heck, even love you). Mission.org. https://medium.com/the-mission/14-things-that-will-make-people-like-you-heck-even-love-you-e0562f5bd72a

Kassel, G., & Jones, A. (2020, April 15). 10 signs you're in an intimate relationship, according to experts. Women's Health. https://www.womenshealthmag.com/sex-and-love/a32007484/intimate-relationship/

Katherine, C. (2022, April 5). Social connectedness and mental health benefits. Bright Futures Psychiatry. https://www.brightfuturespsychiatry.com/social-connectedness-and-mental-health-benefits/

Komer, R. (2021, February 21). Building relational connections. The Center for Family Transformation. https://www.familytransformation.com/2021/02/21/building-relational-connections/

MSD. (2018). Social connectedness and wellbeing - Ministry of Social Development. https://www.msd.govt.nz/about-msd-and-our-work/publications-resources/literature-reviews/social-connectedness-and-wellbeing.html

Komar, M. (2016, June 29). Signs you're making A bad first impression. Bustle. https://www.bustle.com/articles/169879-11-signs-youre-making-a-bad-first-impression-how-to-fix-the-problem

Taylor, R. A. (2022). Making a Great First Impression: The ultimate guide to making a great first impression. Independently Published.

Waggoner, S. C. (1983). First impressions. Child Care Quarterly, 12(4), 247–257. https://doi.org/10.1007/bf01115467

Waters, S. (n.d.). How to make a good first impression: Expert tips and tricks. Betterup.com. https://www.betterup.com/blog/how-to-make-a-good-first-impression

Zenn, J. (2022, September 21). How to make a good first impression: 14 tips to try. HubSpot. https://blog.hubspot.com/marketing/first-impression-tips

10 positive body language techniques to help you succeed. (2021, June 17). Udemy Blog. https://blog.udemy.com/positive-body-language/

Facial expression. (2016, September 30). Facial Palsy UK. https://www.facialpalsy.org.uk/support/patient-guides/facial-expression/

Nonverbal communication: body language and tone of voice. (2020, October 22). Raising Children Network. https://raisingchildren.net.au/toddlers/connecting-communicating/communicating/nonverbal-communication

Positive Body Language - Quick Guide. (n.d.). Tutorialspoint.com. https://www.tutorialspoint.com/positive_body_language/positive_body_language_quick_guide.htm

(N.d.-a). Indeed.com. https://www.indeed.com/career-advice/career-development/body-language-examples

(N.d.-b). Toppr.com. https://www.toppr.com/ask/question/facial-expressions-gestures-eye-contact-nodding-the-head-and-physical-appearances-are-the-form-of/

25 killer actions to boost your self-confidence. (2007, December 10). Zen Habits. https://zenhabits.net/25-killer-actions-to-boost-your-self-confidence/

Khan, S. A. (2020, September 18). Examples of showing respect to others & why it's important? Legacy Business Cultures. https://legacycultures.com/examples-of-showing-respect-to-others-and-its-importance-in-life/

Kloppers, M. (n.d.). 9 clever ways to gain confidence. Mentalhelp.net. https://www.mentalhelp.net/blogs/9-clever-ways-to-gain-confidence/

Notebook, A. (2018, June 28). Three benefits of self-esteem during social interactions. Alison's Notebook - Inspiring The Better You. https://alisonsnotebook.com/why-self-esteem-advantage/

Website, N. H. S. (n.d.). Raising low self-esteem. Nhs.uk. https://www.nhs.uk/mental-health/self-help/tips-and-support/raise-low-self-esteem/

(N.d.). Inc.com. https://www.inc.com/business-insider/how-to-become-more-charasmatic-according-to-psychological-research.html

Brown, J. (2015, June 10). Seven ways to increase your charisma. Entrepreneur. https://www.entrepreneur.com/leadership/ways-to-increase-your-charisma/247075

McKay, K. (2021, November 28). The three elements of charisma: Presence. The Art of Manliness; Art of Manliness. https://www.artofmanliness.com/people/social-skills/the-3-elements-of-charisma-presence/

Business Insider. (2019, March 1). Here are 16 psychological tricks to immediately make people like you more. ScienceAlert. https://www.sciencealert.com/here-are-16-psychological-tricks-to-immediately-make-people-like-you-more

Cherry, K. (2005, November 4). Psychological Persuasion Techniques. Verywell Mind. https://www.verywellmind.com/how-to-become-a-master-of-persuasion-2795901

Clerke, A. S., & Heerey, E. A. (2021). The influence of similarity and mimicry on decisions to trust. Collabra. Psychology, 7(1), 23441. https://doi.org/10.1525/collabra.23441

Cuddy, A. J. C., Kohut, M., & Neffinger, J. (2013). Connect, then lead. Harvard Business Review, 91(7-8), 54-61, 132. https://hbr.org/2013/07/connect-then-lead

Buggy, P. (2017, August 11). Non-Judgment: What is it? And Why Does it Matter? (4 Benefits). Mindful Ambition. https://mindfulambition.net/non-judgment/

Harris, D. W. (2022, March 31). The art of listening in six simple steps. Canadian Mental Health Association. https://www.mentalhealthweek.ca/the-art-of-listening-in-six-steps/

Sutton, J. (2016, July 21). Active listening: The art of empathetic conversation. Positivepsychology.com. https://positivepsychology.com/active-listening/

The fine art of listening can transform the quality of your communication and relationships. (n.d.). Mentalhelp.net. https://www.mentalhelp.net/relationships/listening/

03-26-, U. (2016, March 26). Ten tips for asking good questions. Dummies. https://www.dummies.com/article/business-careers-money/careers/job-searches/ten-tips-for-asking-good-questions-172698/

Dahl, M. (2017, June 14). People will like you more if you ask them questions. The Cut. https://www.thecut.com/2017/06/people-will-like-you-more-if-you-ask-them-questions.html

Hsieh, C., Andrews, T., & Varina, R. (2019, November 20). 100 questions that'll help you *really* get to know someone. Cosmopolitan.

https://www.cosmopolitan.com/sex-love/a29774929/questions-to-get-to-know-someone/

Martel, M. (2013, June 5). How to be amazingly good at asking questions. Lifehack. https://www.lifehack.org/articles/communication/how-amazingly-good-asking-questions.html

Musselwhite, C., & Plouffe, T. (2012, November 12). To have the most impact, ask the right questions. Harvard Business Review. https://hbr.org/2012/11/to-have-the-most-impact-ask-qu

Scuderi, R. (2013, April 10). 11 tips to help improve your active listening skills. Lifehack. https://www.lifehack.org/articles/communication/active-listening-a-skill-that-everyone-should-master.html

Corporativa, I. (2021, April 22). Personal development: unleash your full potential and achieve your goals. Iberdrola. https://www.iberdrola.com/talent/personal-development-tips

Cuncic, A. (2013, August 30). How to be a better storyteller when you are socially anxious. Verywell Mind. https://www.verywellmind.com/how-to-be-a-better-storyteller-3024850

Cuncic, A. (2022, August 31). How to be more interesting. Verywell Mind. https://www.verywellmind.com/how-to-be-more-interesting-6455914

Latumahina, D. (2007, November 14). 4 reasons why curiosity is important and how to develop it. Lifehack. https://www.lifehack.org/articles/productivity/4-reasons-why-curiosity-is-important-and-how-to-develop-it.html

(N.d.-a). Inc.com. https://www.inc.com/travis-bradberry/8-habits-of-incredibly-interesting-people.html

(N.d.-b). Indeed.com. https://www.indeed.com/career-advice/career-development/learn-new-skills

Brandon, J. (2014, May 29). 10 simple ways to make people like you more. Time. https://time.com/135945/make-people-like-you/

Lebowitz, S. (2020, October 19). 15 psychological tricks to make people like you immediately. Independent. https://www.independent.co.uk/life-style/sixteen-psychological-tricks-people-like-you-a7967861.html

Perry, E. (n.d.). How to make people like you: 10 tips to make new friends. Betterup.com. https://www.betterup.com/blog/how-to-make-people-like-you

Lebowitz, S. (2019, March 21). 14 things you're doing that make people instantly dislike you. Business Insider. https://africa.businessinsider.com/strategy/14-things-youre-doing-that-make-people-instantly-dislike-you/rp4xfnf#article

Dawson, K. (2021, February 18). 10 dos and don'ts of starting a new relationship. Brides. https://www.brides.com/starting-a-new-relationship-5105367

Davenport, B. (2021, August 11). Wondering "why don't people like me?" 21 reasons and solutions. Live Bold and Bloom; Barrie Davenport. https://liveboldandbloom.com/08/self-awareness/why-people-dont-like-me

Printed in Great Britain
by Amazon